SAVE YOUR
CITY

How **toxic culture** kills
community & what to do about it

DIANE KALEN-SUKRA

Cover design: Dolce Vita Design

Tellwell Talent
www.tellwell.ca

ISBN
978-0-2288-1272-2 (Hardcover)
978-0-2288-1087-2 (Paperback)
978-0-2288-1086-5 (eBook)

TESTIMONIALS

Save Your City is an inspired and powerful must-read. Our democracy is in peril and this book delivers the right message, by the right person, at the right time.

—IRA BASEN, CBC Radio Producer

I applaud Diane Kalen-Sukra for devising a blueprint for community change. Every community leader should read Save Your City—pen in hand—and then emphatically implement the strategies.

—DR. LEW BAYER, Civility Experts Worldwide

Save Your City is a brilliant book. Practical, grounded in historical lessons, provocative, and right on. This is a timely wake-up call to action for all of us who act and live our values. Civility and respect for the golden rule are not dead. Enjoy this must-read.

—SEAN MAGENNIS,
former YPO Global President & COO

Save Your City is an absolute must-read for civic leaders. Diane Kalen-Sukra masterfully enlightens us on the challenges of modern governance with the wisdom of classical antiquity to address our increasingly uncivil society.

—GEORGE B. CUFF,
Governance & Management Consultant

In loving memory of my late husband Jerome. His legacy lives on in our family tapestry—Victoria, Alexander, Isabel and Sophia. For the journey ahead, guided, as always, by His light.

Table of Contents

·····

Foreword 9

Introduction 13

Part 1: Welcome to Bullyville **19**

   1: CITY GATES 21

   2: SURVIVING UNCIVIL SOCIETY 37

Part 2: Journey to Sustainaville **57**

   3: SANCTUARY 59

   4: JOIN THE RENAISSANCE 81

   5: ONE SHIP, ONE DESTINY 99

Part 3: Sustainable Culture **121**

   6: GLOBAL CALL FOR VALUES
      EDUCATION 123

   7: LOVE IS THE GREATEST CIVIC
      VIRTUE 141

Appendix: ROADMAP TO RENEWING CIVIC
        CULTURE 163

Acknowledgments 165

Endnotes 169

Index 175

FOREWORD

Love your neighbour. Is this just a good idea? Or one that is critical to our survival? Is it just a moral way to live, perhaps to earn favour with whatever deity one may or may not believe in? Or might it be an articulation of the deep wisdom found in antiquity that describes how the universe, including us humans, are designed to work?

In other words, is 'love your neighbour' optional? Or is it as crucial as the air we breathe?

I met the author of this book, Diane Kalen-Sukra, fifteen years ago when she and her family were part of a church where I was the minister. I quickly realized that she was not a typical congregational member, but had conviction, passion, and a vision for the flourishing and well-being of people and communities. (Let me let you in on a little secret: some religious

9

people access their religious communities for comfort and affirmation, but strenuously avoid life-transformation that might generate new change and well-being for our world.)

Kalen-Sukra's conviction has borne obvious fruit in her work where she demonstrates innovative and life-giving leadership in municipal governance and community building. In my view, her success can be attributed in large part to the fact that she has a vision for *why* towns and cities exist, not just a handle on *how* they work.

This book, *Save Your City,* is a wake-up call to us all. Kalen-Sukra argues persuasively that, at a societal level, any further delay in intentionally addressing toxic culture could be fatal to our ability to confront the mounting challenges facing our communities and our nations.

As an ordained minister, I have seen all too often the dangers of not heeding signs and warnings both in our spiritual life and in our practical life. We see today levels of anger and incivility towards one another that have reached proportions we could not have imagined. The erosion of our social fabric—made worse by some of the negative effects of social media—and the mounting fear all around us is stunning. This is especially surprising here in Canada, considering we live in one of the richest and safest nations in the world, with public healthcare and comparatively strong social service supports.

We should be happier.

We should be nicer to each other.

Why aren't we?

Save Your City makes a compelling argument that democracy cannot thrive without a culture of informed, civic-minded, and civic-hearted citizens to support it. To this end, we are taken on a treasure-filled journey through classical antiquity to extract wisdom and experience found in the intellectual and moral traditions that gave birth to democracy and sought to preserve it. This wisdom is then masterfully applied to today's realities, providing direction for individuals, organizations, and communities to chart a new course—a sustainable, life-giving culture.

I work in an organization that houses and cares for refugees when they first arrive in Canada. They flee their homes because their neighbourhood, city, or country has descended into the chaos of violence that destroys human life. Through their eyes, I know that if we do not choose to live well, for the sake of one another and in order to bless one another, eventually what starts as incivility leads to something much worse.

Now is not the time to despair or to withdraw into self-protective modes that guard our own power and well-being. In the end, it is the acts of ordinary people who imagine a better future and who iterate towards it each and every day that will save us. The good wizard Gandalf in *Lord of the Rings* encouraged his small despairing group wisely: "Some believe it is only great power that can hold evil in check, but that is not what I have found. It is the small everyday deeds of ordinary folk that keep the darkness at bay."

This book is an anthem to this ancient wisdom and practice as it applies to sustainable community building and local government. I have served in the faith-based non-profit sector my whole life and have worked to find the light where there is compassion, love, and genuine community. If many of us march in this same direction in the various spaces and sectors in which we live and work, we can sow new life into the narrative of our common life—a sustainable future for us all.

It starts with loving our neighbour.

SAM CHAISE

Executive Director, Christie Refugee Welcome Centre
Former Executive Director, Canadian Baptist Ministries

Toronto, Ontario
January 2019

INTRODUCTION

"So, let's make the most of this beautiful day. Since we're together, we might as well say: Would you be mine? Could you be mine? Won't you be my neighbor?"

This sentimental appeal to community building and neighbourliness was authored in 1967 by educator and entertainer Fred Rogers for his public television series *Mister Rogers' Neighborhood*. He sang these verses, which were broadcast into the homes of generations of children starting in Canada, and then also the United States for over thirty years. His emphasis on loving one's neighbour, sharing and cooperating, celebrating human differences, and cherishing community was not accidental.

Fred Rogers was incredibly intentional, almost crusade-like, about fostering healthy culture by teaching values and emotional management skills in children. He saw this type of education as vital to our ability to live well together. A Presbyterian minister with a focus on child development, he expressed alarm at the fighting and poor behaviour modeled in commercialized children's programming and sought to influence the next generation for the better.

In this age of incivility, disconnectedness, and violence, the wisdom and foresight of Fred Rogers' message is hitting home. A documentary on his life and guiding philosophy aptly called *Won't You Be My Neighbor?* was released in the United States in June 2018 and became the highest-grossing biographical documentary of all time.

Only four months later, the unthinkable happened in Fred Rogers' actual neighbourhood of Squirrel Hill, Pittsburgh. It was October 27, 2018, on the Jewish Sabbath, that holy day of rest and community connection, when a gunman opened fire in the sanctuary of the Tree of Life Synagogue. The twenty-minute murderous rampage is considered the deadliest attack against the Jewish community in American history.

How many times can we say "never again"?

It would be wrong to write off this tragedy as an isolated act of violence. Not when hate crimes in Canada surged forty-seven percent in 2017[1]. Not when there is, on average, a school shooting every week of the year in the United States and epidemic levels of violence and bullying in Canadian schools.[2] Not when mental health issues affect almost twenty percent of

North Americans with increases in suicide and major depressive episodes in youth and a full-scale opioid overdose death march. Not when disconnection, social isolation, and loneliness are national health crises. Not when workplace culture is so toxic that unprecedented numbers of people medicate just to go to work. Not when public discourse, from town halls to online platforms, often reaches beyond incivility into straight-up hatefulness. Not when reports of dysfunctional local governments or "toxic towns" are frequent newspaper headlines.[3]

We are seeing a rise in communities characterized by fear-based cultures of division, relentless comparison and competition, scapegoating, demonizing others, jealousy, and malicious gossip. These are places where: neighbours and "friends" are suspicious of each other or tear each other down, rather than build each other up; bonds are built on common "enemies" and personal advantage, rather than a common purpose to advance the well-being of all; and bullying, intimidation, or shaming to get one's way—whether it be in the playground, workplace or in the public square—goes unchecked by bystanders.

Toxic culture drives folks to seek their own private solutions to the social crisis and related economic and political challenges. This, however, is the very time when we need to build our muscle and capacity to work together to innovate and create solutions to the complex problems we collectively face. These problems include climate change, the infrastructure deficit crisis, ever-growing economic disparity and poverty, the need for affordable housing, and the list goes on.

In the chaos, we are all losing sight of the great threat this toxicity poses to our democratic way of life—our local democracies.

Democracy is not something we have by divine right. It is a hard-won privilege granted to us by those who came before us and fought for it. These were people who knew the tyranny and injustice of oppressive masters who would deny ordinary people a voice and basic human rights, such as freedom of expression and association. But we forget that democracy requires an active, informed, and engaged citizenry that seeks the well-being of all, not just their gang, in order to thrive.

To protect and advance this common good, this book calls on civil society representatives—community leaders, citizens, business leaders, and all who care about fostering healthy communities—to lead a renaissance of democratic values, ideas, and civic education. Just like the last renaissance, this book draws wisdom from the well of classical antiquity, our rich Western democratic tradition, to enrich our understanding of the art of living and working well together in democratic communities.

We live in a sea of culture shapers—from the music industry to marketers. Just like Fred Rogers, we need to be as intentional about culture as the commercial interests that feed on our pocket books and ultimately our souls. Culture is not just something that happens to us. It's something that we choose. We must choose wisely.

To this end, you are further asked in this book to join the global call for a culture and values revolution. The aim is to foster a culture and a future that champions compassion and *agapeic* or unconditional love for each other, all living things, and our environment. Why? Because love and compassion are the twin life forces that have the greatest potential to empower us to save ourselves, our cities, and our world.

Values determine behaviour. Together they form culture. Culture is the engine that sustains us.

This way to Sustainaville!

PART ONE

WELCOME TO BULLYVILLE

1
......

CITY GATES

The most pressing environmental problem we face today is not climate change. Rather it is pollution in the public square, where a smog of adversarial rhetoric, propaganda and polarization stifles discussion and debate, creating resistance to change and thwarting our ability to solve our collective problems.

—James Hoggan, David Suzuki Foundation Chair
Author of *I'm Right and You're an Idiot*

"I no longer feel compelled to work for the community," said a rural mayor with a likeness to St. Nick in his very public mid-term 2018 resignation letter. "I actually feel ill every time I return to town and sick to my stomach to attend council meetings. I am not able to sleep at night due to worrying because of the divisiveness. It is affecting my health, and I won't suffer any longer."

This resignation, which the mayor stated was due to the actions and behaviour of "a certain portion of the community" that had "poisoned the workings of council," was followed by the resignations of two other municipal council members.

What made the mayor's resignation especially troubling was the fact that he had diligently served the same community for thirty years, fourteen years as an elected representative— the only thing that had changed was *political culture over time.* Like the canary in the mine, he grew weary from the toxic fumes. The end result? An experienced leader was lost, the governance and effectiveness of a local government were shaken, and a community was left behind, further divided.

If this was the experience of only one or two or even a handful of communities with unique governance challenges or social issues, it could be chalked up as personally tragic for those involved. The trouble is we are seeing a sharp rise in incivility and bullying in our communities *everywhere*, stifling democratic debate, paralyzing municipal councils, costing precious resources and tax dollars, and hampering the proper and effective functioning of local government.

A 1946 documentary made by *Encyclopedia Britannica* in collaboration with Yale University to educate citizens after the war about the importance of guarding and preserving their local democracies nicely sums up why this is a problem for all of us: "What happens in a single community is the problem of its own citizens. But it is also the problem of us all because as communities go, so goes the nation."[4]

ENTER AT YOUR OWN RISK

And so goes the nation indeed. Municipal politics today is too often characterized by shocking and very public breaches of acceptable conduct by elected officials, staff, and citizens. Barely a day goes by without another damning headline:

> COUNCILLORS BEHAVING BADLY
>
> TOXIC COUNCIL RELATIONSHIPS DAMAGING THE TOWN
>
> HARASSMENT REPORT PROVES CITY HAS WORKPLACE CULTURE PROBLEM
>
> ANGRY GROUP CONFRONTS CAO AT HOME
>
> CAO CHARGED WITH DEFRAUDING TOWN
>
> MAYOR APPEALS TO VOTERS AFTER REVIEW FINDS HE HARASSED, BULLIED FEMALE STAFF
>
> CAO RESIGNS OVER COUNCIL BEHAVIOUR
>
> DELAY IN ADDRESSING WORKPLACE RACISM 'SLAP IN THE FACE' SAYS COUNCILLOR
>
> TOXIC CITY HALL LED BY 'PARANOID' MAYOR

That's only a small sample of recent Canadian headlines and doesn't include the heightened shenanigans—such as accusations of voter fraud, defamation, vandalism, and theft among other toxic actions in the public square—that transpire during local elections.

Besides eroding public trust and creating costly organizational paralysis, this toxicity is an unhealthy development for our local democracies. We know the quality and diversity of candidates running for office suffer, for the less socially secure you are, the less likely you are to subject yourself to the politics of the snake pit. Existing and experienced politicians are deterred from seeking a second term. Low voter turnout is chronic, with about a quarter of eligible US city voters and about half of Canadian eligible city voters casting a ballot. The situation only worsens as media outlets are consolidated and local news coverage diminishes. And election by acclamation remains high. Many jurisdictions have more positions filled by acclamation than by elections.

"We need an active democracy and active citizens to solve these problems," says CEO Craig Pollett of the Municipalities of Newfoundland and Labrador where elections by acclamation are over fifty-five percent. In the most recent elections, a quarter of all provincial municipalities had to extend their nomination period because there were no candidates coming forward to fill vacant seats. "Nobody's coming to solve these problems for these towns; they need to find solutions themselves. One of the ways you do that is by engaging in a healthy debate around policies and direction. That's the role elections play."[5]

The challenges facing communities and local governments today are formidable. In days gone by, when resources seemed abundant, public trust was high, continual expansion of services was an expected norm, and citizens were (for the most part) somewhere between happy and complacent.

Today, the reality is very different. Heightened pressures and challenges include a ballooning infrastructure deficit; critical infrastructure at or near the end of its life; public trust at an all-time low; the retirement of waves of experienced municipal employees, leaving operational vacuums; the declining activity of civil society associations and volunteerism; an increasingly stringent regulatory environment; greater economic disparity; unprecedented financial pressures; an affordable housing crisis; a mental health crisis; the accumulation of increased responsibilities on municipalities; lack of public understanding of the role, resources and processes of local government; heightened public expectations for engagement and involvement in decision-making; and the need to prepare for climate change, including straining local resources to manage today's wind storms, flooding, and wildfires.

These are all complex problems that require community leadership, innovation, collaboration, and consistency to address, all of this at the very time when we seem to have lost the art of living and working well together to accomplish our common goals.

DIMMING DEMOCRATIC LIGHTS

The very fact that it is popular nowadays to preface all types of civic and organizational activity—including business activity—with the word "sustainable" is an acknowledgments that our current course is, at best, missing the mark if not headed towards an even greater crisis. We have sustainable community building, sustainable leadership, sustainable employment, sustainable living, sustainable growth, sustainable development, sustainable economy, sustainable living, and the list goes on.

This trend is a polite, non-threatening way to admit what the renowned author and evangelist of healthy communities, Jane Jacobs, prophetically argues in her 2004 book, *Dark Age Ahead*. Namely, our cities are on the brink of a new dark age, a period of what she calls "cultural collapse".

Jacobs writes that this is evidenced in the serious decay of key pillars of a stable, democratic society, including the decline of the family and households due to unbearable economic and social pressures, the rise of consumerism and individualism, and the transformation of education into mere credentialism. She is no longer a lone voice.

In his 2018 New Year's message, Canadian bestselling author of *Deepening Community: Building Communities that Sustain Us*, Paul Born asks: "As we enter into another chaotic year, do we dare optimism? Or, do we embrace a growing sense that it is too late? Should we just let things unravel, focus on what is best for Me, and watch it all come tumbling down?"[6]

Born sounds the alarm bell on the shallow substitutes that now stand in the place of deep meaningful community connection. An obligatory Facebook "like" rather than a meaningful get-together or dinner. Or worse, the rise of fear-based communities, dangerous places that thrive on the creation of enemies or developing an "us vs. them" mentality where animosity, isolation, and threats between neighbours are the norm, rather than neighbourly cooperation and enhancement.

The signs in civil society are everywhere—the decline in the vitality or even the existence of many service clubs and organizations, the loss of purpose and governance challenges in so many non-profit groups, and the difficulty inspiring or recruiting community members into action. Of course, there are many exceptions, but the trend is undeniable.

Harvard professors and political scientists Stephen Levistky and Daniel Ziblat have, after years of studying the fall of democracies around the world, felt the need to turn their attention to home soil. In their 2018 book *How Democracies Die*, they express their alarm at the prevalence of key indicators of collapse, including the increasing hostility in public discourse and weakening of critical institutional buffers in the face of heightening social, economic, and environmental challenges.

They warn us of that litmus test of the decline of democracy—the one where the legitimacy of one's opponents is denied. We see this happening everywhere, from national politics down to local politics in small rural communities throughout Canada and the United States.

"Authoritarian politicians cast their rivals as criminal, subversive, unpatriotic, or a threat to national security or the existing way of life," says Levistky. "The drift into authoritarianism doesn't always set off alarm bells. Citizens are often slow to realize that their democracy is being dismantled even as it happens before their eyes."[7]

DANGEROUS LULLABY

Jane Jacobs warns us not to fall into the "mass amnesia" that characterizes the descent into a Dark Age where people forget and fail to understand what they have lost and, therefore, fail to fight to preserve it. She notes during the last Dark Age, "not only was most classical culture forgotten", but also citizenship gave way to serfdom and feudal relations as the people sunk into poverty, ignorance, and squalor. In the final days before Western Rome's collapse, "local governments had been expunged by imperial decree and were replaced by centralized military despotism."[8]

Today, we are once again seeing local governments that are unable to govern themselves effectively. In the United States, over sixty municipalities have gone bankrupt in the past few years alone. Entire democratically elected city councils are essentially fired, and administrators are put in place to manage the municipality. In Australia, over a hundred Australian municipalities have been consolidated because they could not effectively manage their public assets and sustainably deliver services.

Governance collapse in Canadian municipalities is also happening, despite a robust financial reporting system and regulatory environment that sets limits on how much debt municipalities can take on and forbids running operating deficits. Mid-term and often cluster resignations of council members have become a disturbing and growing trend, which results in some councils not having a quorum to make decisions, not to mention the disruption and cost of holding by-elections. The investigations into widely publicized corruption in Quebec municipalities led to some—including the province's third largest city—being put under trusteeship. Misconduct included behaviour so antithetical to public service, such as verbal abuse, arbitrary suspensions, conflict of interest and intrusions into the private lives of employees, that one can't be blamed for losing hope.

Municipalities on the verge of governance collapse, don't always look so on the outside. What the public doesn't necessarily see is the gap between mandated legislative requirements and the internal capacity of the administration to deliver given the tsunami of pressures on councils and administrations that is only intensifying. Internal conflict, toxic councils and polarized communities make matters so much worse. And like an organism, these three affect each other. Even if a local government is doing the right thing, for instance, the cultural conditions, public understanding and heart of the people may be such that they don't appreciate those efforts and may even actively seek to undermine them. Hope rests in the crack where the light shines through. In democratic societies, that is the time and place when a community awakens to the fact that it is collectively responsible for its own destiny.

This experience led me over time to think deeply about the nature of cultural transformation in democratic societies and to review the wisdom of our rich Western democratic community building tradition. The Athenian lawmaker Solon, who is credited with paving the way for democracy, used poetry to lament and warn of the city being under threat from the unrestrained greed and arrogance of its citizens. Greek philosopher Plato told us that the city is what it is because the citizens are what they are. The French aristocrat and political philosopher Alexis de Tocqueville prescribed a "new political science" that considers the importance of maintaining and fostering the right *mores*, or *habits of the heart* for democratic societies to remain healthy and just.

The great culture shapers today are the entertainment and marketing industries—from the shows we watch, to the music we listen to, and the lifestyle shaping advertisements. However, these industries are accountable to no one, except their shareholders.

Too often, driving sales easily and quickly involves appealing to consumers' simplest appetites and ensuring that citizens see themselves as *little more than consumers*, whose civic expression in the public square is *little more than shopping well*. For instance, virtually every human civilization has understood that inciting envy is unwise and divisive, yet marketers regularly encourage us to "make your neighbours jealous" by the purchasing the latest patio set or new car. Values expressed in behaviour becomes culture—a fact we ignore at our great peril.

Democracy's traditional counterbalance to misinformation, manipulation and apathy was the free press—that truth-telling, fact-sorting machinery that keep the people free and independent by providing hard research, critical thinking, and quality information to the people. Unfortunately, the current state of media ownership, concentrated as it is in ever fewer hands and operating under market pressures that centralize news outlets, means that comprehensive news coverage of local issues is quickly becoming a thing of the past. Research shows that civic engagement, including voting in local elections, is higher where there is local municipal news coverage.

The Public Policy Forum, a non-profit think tank in Ottawa showed in a recent report titled *Mind the Gaps* that city hall reporting has declined by thirty-eight percent in twenty small and mid-sized Canadian cities from 2008 to 2017. The decline is just as dramatic in the United States and the United Kingdom. To this end, the BBC is funding "local democracy reporters". In the US, private foundations have promised $20 million to help local news organizations become "sustainable". In Canada, $50 million was committed to be spent over five years in the 2018 federal budget to "support local journalism across the country" with a recommendation that news agencies be made eligible for non-profit status. [9]

American political commentator and journalist Bill Moyers succinctly describes the quality of democracy and the quality of journalism as "deeply intertwined".

TOCQUEVILLE'S NIGHTMARE

In my opinion, the main evil of the present democratic institutions of the United States does not arise . . . from their weakness, but from their strength . . . I am not so much alarmed at the excessive liberty which reigns in that country as at the inadequate securities which one finds there against tyranny.

Alexis de Tocqueville *Democracy in America*

We can't say we haven't been warned about the importance of culture in fostering healthy and well-governed democratic communities. We were explicitly warned of this almost 200 years ago in a most compelling and comprehensive way by the French aristocrat and civil servant Alexis de Tocqueville in his classic work *Democracy in America*.

At this time, when we are at risk of succumbing to the fog of a new Dark Age, losing track of the cultural norms on which our society was built, Tocqueville's writings provide us with a rare opportunity to look with the same wonder and appreciation as he did on the democratic project, which we too often take for granted today. His observations make it clear that **a toxic culture is detrimental, if not fatal, to a thriving democracy.**

Alexis de Tocqueville came to North America in 1831 and travelled for nine months, from settlements in Upper and Lower Canada (Quebec and Ontario today) to southern townships in the United States, to seek out as he writes in his introduction, "the image of democracy itself, with its inclinations, its character, its prejudices and its passions." He described the democratic revolution as a *providential fact* and reasoned that it was hundreds of years in the making, since the very idea of the equal worth and dignity of every human being was unleashed in the ancient world.

Today, this idea that all men are created equal and worthy is one that we take as *self-evident,* but it wasn't always so.

Perhaps the recognition of this *providential fact* explains why this aristocrat, whose grandfather was executed in the French Revolution, and whose father only narrowly escaped the same fate, would depart from the resistance to democracy of his class and pursue a curiosity that sought, through examination, to show how expressions of free people in democratic societies—from their townships to their associations and the culture fostered—contributed to its thriving or its demise. He wanted to take lessons back to France to ensure the democracy that was taking form in Europe would learn from its more advanced cousin in North America.

His observations include fascinating comparisons between the nature and pitfalls of aristocratic societies and democratic societies. He notes that the powerful and wealthy in aristocratic society can achieve great common undertakings on their own; the populace need not combine in order to act. In contrast, people in democratic societies acquired what he calls the *habit of forming associations* in virtually every sphere of life—professional, social, civil, and political—out of necessity, without which common goals could not be achieved, and their "independence would be in great jeopardy."

In a way, Tocqueville is saying that democratic local governments and the voluntary associations and societies formed in thriving democracies are what define the social, political, and economic order and prevent local democracies from becoming dysfunctional or tyrannical.

This habit of free peoples to set up townships (municipalities) and associations everywhere there was a settlement was one of the features of democracies that impressed Tocqueville the most. Losing this habit, was one of the great threats to democracy he identified. He sees local government as important—the very field where justice and individual freedoms can be secured or lost. He writes that "the health of a democratic society may be measured by the quality of functions performed by private citizens."

Today, we may sum up this lesson thus: *a healthy democracy requires active, informed and engaged citizens.*

Other *mores* (or habits of the heart), however, led people in democratic societies to act in ways that were culturally antithetical to community well-being and could lead to Tocqueville's dreaded nightmare: *the tyranny of the majority.*

For instance, he noticed that democratic cultures tend to use the principle of equality as a levelling force to cut down the talented, the wise, and the good, which has the effect of fostering a culture of mediocrity. While in aristocratic societies birth established status and fortune, however unjustly, the opposite in democratic societies stirred in its people a restlessness and "strange melancholy often haunting the inhabitants of democracies in the midst of abundance."[10] He argues that when a citizen in a democratic society is unable to achieve the greatness he or she feels they ought to, envy and ill will are more easily stirred up to relieve themselves of any shame they may feel and satisfy their belief that one must at least be equal to their neighbours.

A most disturbing habit of the heart that Tocqueville identified was a lack of social courage and critical thinking in the face of the pressure of public opinion. There are few places, he writes, where one could witness "less independence of mind, and true freedom of discussion." He observed people more willing to engage in conversations filled with shallow niceties than risk, in this commercial society, offending their neighbour with whom they may one day wish to do business.

Tocqueville quotes from American founding father James Madison to warn us of how this tyranny of the majority can undermine justice and civil society:

> *Justice is the end of government. It is the end of civil society. It ever has been and ever will be pursued until it be obtained, or until liberty be lost in the pursuit. In a society under the forms of which the stronger faction can readily unite and oppress the weaker, anarchy may as truly be said to reign as in a state of nature, where the weaker individual is not secured against the violence of the stronger.*[11]

The philosophers of Ancient Greece all argued the same— namely that the ideal society is a just society. Like every system before it and any system after it, without justice, democracy will fail. Without active, engaged, and informed citizens, it will fail. Without a "good spirit", as Aristotle calls it, that seeks the well-being of all, democracy will fail.

As much as we like to say, "every vote counts," a much richer understanding of what creates and maintains thriving democracies is "every heart counts."

2
. . . . .

SURVIVING UNCIVIL SOCIETY

A person must have something to cling to. Without that we are as a pea vine sprawling in search of a trellis.

—E.B. White

Everybody feels the evil, but no one has the courage or energy enough to seek the cure.

—Alexis de Tocqueville, *Democracy in America*

You can learn a great deal about a society at any given time based on its literature and especially its humour. Successful comedy holds a mirror up to a subject, allowing us to laugh at what might otherwise enrage or upset us or might, in some cases, escape our notice altogether.

Consider Count Olaf the antagonist in the wildly popular series of humorously subversive children's books *A Series of Unfortunate Events,* by Lemony Snicket (AKA Daniel Handler). Olaf is the flamboyant criminal mastermind whose aims throughout the books include getting his hands on the inheritance of the unfortunate Baudelaire orphans—the books' protagonists. He successfully and without shame or conscience, manipulates every public institution, organization, local government, and law enforcement agency, including the ones designed to protect orphans, in his maniacal pursuit of the children's fortune.

The books have sold more than 60 million copies and seen adaptations to both the big screen, with Jim Carey playing Olaf, and the small screen Netflix series, with Neil Patrick Harris playing Olaf. Harris's Olaf encapsulates the character brilliantly during one of his musical numbers entitled "Keep Chasing Your Schemes."

> *You gotta keep chasing your schemes*
> *Keep chasing your schemes*
> *A journey begins with one single step*
> *To get to the end*
> *You gotta schlep, schlep, schlep*
> *Your goals are like a sapphire*
> *Watch it as it gleams*
> *You gotta keep chasing your schemes*

Ne'er-do-wells like Olaf or *The Simpson's* Mr. Burns are entertaining because they are unmasked versions of folks we recognize. You don't have to be demonizing and defrauding innocent orphans to fall into self-interested, end-focused thinking and scheming. The beauty of Count Olaf is that he's upfront about it. He tells us flat out that he's not chasing *dreams*, just *schemes*.

The seventh book of the thirteen-book series is entitled *The Vile Village*, and in it the hapless Baudelaire children seek sanctuary in a rural township, named VFD (which it turns out stands for Village of Fowl Devotees). Its deranged and conformist citizens are ruled by officious community leaders who salivate at the prospect of persecuting and punishing anyone who violates any of the numerous nonsensical laws or norms. The punishment, for instance, for putting more than fifteen pieces of nuts on a hot fudge sundae is the death penalty. Needless to say, the Village provided no protection for the Baudelaires, rather the villagers sought only to exploit the vulnerable orphans and ultimately endanger them further.

The book is a chilling and extreme illustration of Tocqueville's tyranny of the majority in action. Even the author muses in the introduction that he wonders why anyone should want to read such a dreadful tale, recounting "each dismal moment of [the orphans'] stay in V.F.D."

Perhaps the millions of children and young adults who are reading or watching this series on television and the movie theatres are doing so for more than just the comedy.

SHATTERED SOCIAL CONTRACT

Some people are born with a profession or a career in mind. This vision never came to me. My parents were mortified when, in university, I switched out of commerce to pursue studies in political science and philosophy, especially when a good business degree could provide a tight-knit immigrant Greek family, one that had faced economic hardship, with hope and a brighter future.

"Diana, you're a woman," my Dad would reason with me in his heavy Greek accent. "You cannot be a philosopher." He expressed this sentiment with the heartbreak of a parent telling their daughter that the coach won't let her play on the only baseball team in town because it's all-boys.

I only heightened my parents' stress and confusion when I explained that I didn't want to be a philosopher. In fact, I didn't want to be anything at all. I just wanted to understand why there was so much injustice in the world, why there were so many wars, and why so many lived in such extreme poverty in the midst of such abundant wealth and resources. I wanted to know who was responsible and why no one felt empowered to stop it. I thought by learning this, I would understand how to live my life. And I had somehow planted in my mind the idea that the answers could be found in the vast university libraries and the great brain trust of wise and knowledgeable university professors.

Several years later, I completed graduate school and did not have any conclusive answers, only a better understanding of how we got here and an appreciation for the thinking of political philosophers and the courage of various political actors throughout history. I still hadn't a clue what I was going to do with my life, but I was certain of two things—that I longed for family and community and didn't belong in the modern university.

While I enjoyed certain areas of political research and writing and may have considered spending some time doing that if it served a worthy purpose, the only types of research which seemed to be approved or supported with university research funds were those of a most unusual and esoteric nature: "The Political Economy of Racialized Okra Farming in Northern Peru" –or– "An Examination of the Dialectical Nature of Identity Politics in Sub-Saharan Africa".

Okay, I'm exaggerating, but not by much.

At the time, I blamed myself for not being cool enough to be satisfied with pouring my efforts into some edgy academic area of study. Recently I learned that my so-called coolness, or lack thereof, was not the problem. A group of professors, Helen Pluckrose, James A. Lindsay, and Peter Boghossian, fed up with some of the work that passed for scholarship nowadays, launched a covert mission to produce and submit for publication under false names and credentials ridiculous studies with faulty and weak analyses and absurd conclusions. One paper, for example, argued that dog parks are Petri-dishes for canine rape culture. Another, is that dildos are tools of social justice. Seven of these submissions were accepted for publication in some of the most prestigious academic journals, including the top academic culture journal, and praised for their "excellent scholarship".

The professors revealed their shockingly successful deception in October 2018, causing world-wide news frenzy. In their view, this type of academia survives under the guise of carrying on with the noble work of the civil rights movement but *actually* subverts it by pushing a "kind of social snake oil onto a public that keeps getting sicker."[12]

Seems my parents were right to be concerned with my liberal arts education after all.

But I was right too. I was right to seek what I now understand to be a thorough civic education at university. Though I pursued it with all my heart and mind, it seemed unfashionable and secondary to all the exciting new fields of study. Though Jane Jacobs has passed on now, I feel this is what she meant when she spoke of the cultural decay inevitable when education is reduced to mere credentialism in democratic societies. A vibrant democracy requires citizens with superior critical thinking skills and a strong moral compass.

It is a responsibility that comes with self-government. Like the entertainment industry and the media, universities are powerful culture shapers. If the PhD academics and editors that approved the seven bogus papers—one which even copied and submitted a section of *Mein Kampf* while making a case for intersectional feminism—did not have the critical thinking skills to recognize that this was not true scholarship, what hope is there for citizens who are mostly busy and fed pre-packaged and polished points of view delivered as fact?

Having found the love of my life, I moved on from academia to my other longing—having a family. While today's generation has the wonderfully subversive *A Series of Unfortunate Events*, my generation grew up on *Mister Rogers' Neighborhood* and *Little House in the Prairie*. What could be sweeter or more rewarding than growing up kids in a loving community, being kind to your neighbour, or joining in on a community barn-raising?

That was the mid-1990s, during a recession in Toronto—a big city where jobs were scarce, and any opening produced thousands of applicants. Even then, getting the job was not the biggest problem; it was the sense of absolute ownership and disposability of the employee in the modern employment relationship. Whatever implicit social contract that may have existed in that master–servant relationship was disappearing. Frank Kelman, former managing director of

Talent Management magazine describes the end of this social contract and the formation of a new one this way:

> *It's not enough for workers to simply show up and work hard, follow the rules and expect to be rewarded . . . [There is] a new social contract. On the one hand employees are looking for dynamic experiences and learning opportunities, sometimes more than a generous salary or benefits package. On the other, employers are looking to quickly capture high-skilled expertise to contribute to an innovation pipeline that will establish an employer brand that keeps their talent attraction cycle moving indefinitely.*[13]

Well, I wasn't ready to be part of an employer's *talent attraction cycle* that moved indefinitely to capture *high-skilled expertise* so that I could *contribute to an innovation pipeline*. During our child-rearing years, we sought the stability and dignity of a good union job in the manufacturing sector as a safe place to be while starting our family. While I was pregnant with our second child, my husband had been laid off due to insufficient work at the steel plant he was working at, and the autoworkers plant I was working at went on strike to resist the twenty percent wage cut the employer sought among other reductions.

The strike dragged on for months in the bitter cold of the winter of 2000. It would take me hours to warm up at home, only to return the next day for another long shift on the picket line. The union's slogan was *fighting back makes a difference*. It was inspiring enough, I suppose.

The dominant narrative of our predicament was most defeating. Namely, our employer was simply a corporation responding to shareholders under hypercompetitive pressures to maximize profits and market share in a globalized economy and there was no political force that was going to change that. And around us we could see one manufacturing community after another gutted by the diminishing investments and plant closures that were ravaging families, communities, and the province—the industrial heartland of Canada.

You could scour the newspapers, listen to national, provincial, and local politicians, and yet there was no plan, shared vision, or even serious dialogue between government and civil society leaders that went beyond the political parties pointing fingers or debating who was hypothetically better at fueling the economy to "provide jobs".

Imagine if disenfranchisement on that scale was caused by a natural disaster, rather than corporations responding to market forces. It would be unfair to expect the government to stop nature, but there are certainly supports, ways to meaningfully express care for people, neighbours and communities and assist with the transition—particularly if the "new normal" was going to be unstable, precarious work. Instead, there was silence and the ever-present message that *you're on your own, society does not owe you or anyone a duty of care.*

Whether we understood it as such at the time or not, it highlighted the erosion of the social contract between the people and their various levels of government. The new logic was that the *invisible hand of the market* was responsible for the devastation of lives and communities, and more importantly, democratic governments at all levels were either impotent or not responsible.

Could this be the fulfillment of Tocqueville's warning that, when you live under a corporate aristocracy, working people will be *impoverished* and *debased* and then *abandoned* when our service is no longer necessary? I bet the almost 15,000 General Motors employees slated to permanently lose their jobs on the continent this year could relate. Tocqueville writes:

> *The territorial aristocracy of former ages was either bound by law, or thought itself bound by usage, to come to the relief of its serving-men and to relieve their distress. But the manufacturing aristocracy of our age first impoverishes and debases the men who serve it and then abandons them . . . I am of the opinion, on the whole, that the manufacturing aristocracy which is growing up under our eyes is one of the harshest that ever existed in the world . . . the friends of democracy should keep their eyes anxiously fixed in this direction; for if ever a permanent inequality of conditions and aristocracy again penetrates into the world, it may be predicted that this is the gate by which they will enter.*[14]

Back at the picket line, the despair was rising. After months of watching executives and managers refusing to negotiate and driving over the hills of the corporate grounds in their

Hummers, rather than face the picket lines at the many entranceways, one of the strikers took matters in his own hands.

It was the first act of dangerous incivility I had ever experienced. In fact, it was criminal. The perpetrator was a quiet, hardworking man and father who was a striking union employee, but he had never really been known as a union supporter. He seemed level headed in every way. I arrived at the picket line to learn he had fashioned a collection of nails and washers into a tiny explosive that he placed on one of the hills where the managers slunk into work. His intentions, apparently, were not to hurt anyone, but to do damage to the company vehicle and to scare the employer. Thankfully, no one was hurt. Needless to say, the consequences for him and his family were severe. Ultimately, the strike was lost, wages cut, and the spirits of long-term employees, in particular, were crushed.

As for the slogan *fighting back makes a difference,* it didn't quite play the same way after that.

Since that day, I have viewed much of the rising incivility we are seeing in society through the lens of that strike—as a reaction to breaches of the social contract; the growing sense that social and economic conditions are only worsening; the feeling of helplessness and disconnectedness that arises from the belief that no one cares or is responsible; the fear that *democracy* is little more than theatre and that voting is ultimately incapable of leading to fundamental change. In his book *Bowling Alone: The Collapse and Revival of American*

Community, Robert Putnam warns us that "people divorced from community, occupation, and association are first and foremost among the supporters of extremism."

The 2008 economic crisis, which resulted in the governments of the people bailing out the banks who caused the crisis, further eroded any sense that the governments of the people had a plan for the long-term well-being of the people. And since then, the challenges facing individuals, communities, municipalities, and the country—from climate change to a mental health crisis—have only intensified.

And incivility is contagious—often spreading by way of righteous indignation until even those without legitimate grievance have come down with symptoms and taken sides. Or to look at it another way, incivility is the social equivalent of CO^2 and leads to a sort of cultural climate change that is very difficult to reverse. Anger, confusion, and a willingness to engage in bullying to get one's way are all results of the current hot house climate we find ourselves in.

Unless we engage and empower citizens through civic education, creative solution brainstorming, the formulation of shared vision, and meaningful action (both individual and organizational) in an attempt to build thriving local economies, workplaces, and communities, there is a lot more incivility that we have yet to experience before a social order is born to channel or contain it.

SHIFTING SANDS

In 1991, my family could not afford to send me to university. I remember staring at my acceptance letter and recognizing that I could have been one of the millions of talented young people in other countries for whom acceptance without sufficient funds meant no schooling. I felt so grateful to live in a democracy that valued equality of opportunity. And I thought about how wise and visionary the people must have been who fought for and created a political and economic system where, even if you were poor, you could still attend university.

My first year was a fully funded experience. By the second year, the government was moving to reduce grant funding and convert it to student loans. At the same time, universities were dramatically increasing their tuition rates. My tuition fees doubled, student loans went up, and though I worked through university, the $6.85 an hour minimum wage didn't begin to make up for the difference.

I graduated as a student debt slave.

As more and more student debt slaves were graduating into a recessionary economy, the Canadian government moved to restrict student debt from being discharged in bankruptcy, joining the ranks of court ordered fines and unpaid child support. Today, Canadian students owe $28 billion in interest accruing government student loans.

The University of Pennsylvania's October 2018 public policy paper titled *The Student Debt Crisis: Could It Slow the US Economy?* documents the negative impact student debt has on the lives and contributions of students to their families, workplaces, and communities. It also reports some startling US statistics—that student debt has more than tripled since 2007, reaching $1.52 trillion in the first quarter of 2018 alone, second only to mortgage debt.

Christopher Peterson, a University of Utah law professor and consumer finance expert, says that the student debt crisis is "changing the culture of America." And indeed, it is.

Graduates spend years paying off student loans to banks, money that could have been spent in the local economy. Who has time to become an active and engaged citizen or join a community association or volunteer when they are working in a gig economy paying off massive student loans and housing costs that require an out-of-reach annual income to afford? How much loving and supportive attention are parents who are that stressed out able to give their kids? Bonds of friendship are undermined as people no longer have time to invest in friends and neighbours. Even pets are developing higher than ever levels of anxiety and other disorders. All of this contributes to our brokenness, our lack of connection, and our lack of time to even establish a shared vision.

My sense of purpose and hope soared when I got a job as a television producer at CBC's flagship political talk show

CounterSpin. The idea behind the show was that the voices on the left and the voices on the right rarely sit down and have a reasoned discussion in the public square—at least not a discussion that involves the citizens. The national town hall-style show was filled to the brim each week night with ordinary citizens, as politicians say, who would watch the discussion and then ask questions before a national audience. It was the ultimate democratic exercise and true to the original mandate of public broadcasters from the BBC, to PBS, and CBC to provide citizens in a democracy with civil discourse and quality information that was free from financial or political interests.

Canadian journalist Sue Gardner and former director of CBC website and online news outlets describes the foundation of the BBC in 1922 in this way:

> *The people who advocated establishing the BBC as a public company—a mix of politicians, businessmen, and civil servants—believed that broadcasting needed to serve the public interest. They believed an informed citizenry was essential to a healthy democracy, and they were living in a period when public faith in government and media had been badly shaken by World War I. They wanted to build social cohesion, and they wanted the poor to have access to education and culture.*[15]

Over time, however, the lofty mandates of public broadcasters were eroded, seemingly precipitated by the never-ending funding cuts, and replaced with a worthy—though decidedly lighter—mandate to support cultural expression and identity through information and entertainment. It was only a matter of time before this town hall-style show that modeled civil public discourse and informed citizen engagement ended. It was replaced with a much "sexier" and entertaining show that executives thought would be more appealing to younger audiences: *George Stroumboulopoulos Tonight* (formerly *The Hour*), bringing viewers "smart, sharp, and intimate conversation with some of the world's biggest stars and original thinkers."

CITY HALL UNDER SIEGE

Like a nesting bird, I found my way back to community building—first as a union representative for municipal workers across Canada in 2003, then as a local government management official in 2013. It was here that I came to deeply understand the magnitude of the crisis facing our local governments and communities. Everywhere budgets were being squeezed, while responsibilities and complexities grew and common ground between interests was getting harder and harder to find.

In 2007, I was assigned to run the coordinated bargaining campaign for the city workers of Vancouver and the surrounding Lower Mainland municipalities. This round of negotiations was contentious because it was the round that would see the cities through the 2010 Olympics. The city workers were understandably frustrated seeing that there was money on the table to host the world, but not to make it affordable for them to live and work in the communities they served. We called it *fairness for civic workers* and launched radio ads broadcasting on all major stations that replicated the old documentary film reel sound and genre, with a heavy male voice describing our condition:

> *Notice the striking similarity in climate and geography of 2010 Olympics host Vancouver and Ancient Olympia. Both cities boast mountainous backdrops, sophisticated irrigation systems, stunning architecture, open markets and festivals. There is, however, one striking difference. While the slaves of Ancient Olympia* **could** *afford to live where they worked, the city workers of Vancouver* **could not.** *Support fairness for civic workers.*

The argument was compelling and undeniable. While it still took the strike to hammer the point home, there was a measure of social unity around this point. The strike resulted in the largest public sector wage increase in memory—just under twenty percent. Through pattern bargaining, this wage increase became the norm across the province in municipalities everywhere. And today, the city of Vancouver is so acutely aware of the affordability problem that affordable housing was a major election issue in the 2018 municipal elections. In January 2019, Demographia International Housing Survey released its annual report which ranked Vancouver housing as the second least-affordable in the world after Hong Kong.

The problem that we face is this: *Who is responsible for this affordability problem? And who pays to fix it?* The sad truth is municipalities really are cash strapped, and there is no wage increase large enough in many cities that can make it affordable for city workers to live where they work.

And in so many ways, city managers and city workers are in this together, serving the same community, the same public good. A strike or a lockout represents a breakdown of discourse and often civility (on either or both sides). Tomas Spath and Cassandra Dahnke, founders of the Institute for Civility in Government write that:

> *Civility is claiming and caring for one's identity, needs and beliefs without degrading someone else's in the process.*[16]

The consequences of a local government labour disruption are onerous for the public. The negative impact on workplace morale and effectiveness—which includes civic service delivery—is often lasting. In my experience, many of these disputes could be avoided if we genuinely understood and lived respect and understanding for each other, love for our community and our noble work as public servants.

At this very time, however, when we need the ability to collaborate and cooperate and innovate together, to find unique sustainable local solutions and creative partnerships through healthy and productive discourse, **culture**—both community and organizational—is becoming more toxic.

Rising incivility, divisiveness, and caustic behaviour are straining relations at the council table, between the council and staff, as well as between citizens and municipal representatives, making positive change and effective action more difficult.

Furthermore, employee audits are presenting data identifying harassment and bullying of civic employees—the very people who deliver vital civic services—to be as high as twenty percent in some communities. Sadly, much of this bullying is also happening between colleagues. During my time as a national union representative involved with numerous workplaces over the years, I experienced in my lifetime the exponential rise in harassment grievances relative to other types of grievances and the breakdown of meaningful solidarity between employees.

Our growing social issues are costing precious municipal tax dollars. These are funds that, if not needed to deal with incivility, social disorder, and mental health, could be invested in our aging infrastructure and service delivery.

While difficult to quantify, some examples include the growing need to: invest in security details to protect politicians; armour up city hall to protect staff from citizens; install safety shields on busses to protect bus drivers; increase training for staff and bylaw enforcement officials on how to deal with distressed and/or mentally ill citizens; increase policing costs to deal with sharp rises in social disorder; and provide dire supports needed to address the growing opioid crisis that is killing thousands. Increasingly, even union offices install security and safety shields to "protect" themselves from their members.

Mental health and social disorder are not only big-city problems. Just ask your local law enforcement officials. The very nature of policing has changed in our communities due to this growing problem.

The National Alliance on Mental Illness reports that one in five Americans experience mental illness in any given year. The Centre for Addiction and Mental Health reports that by the time Canadians reach forty years of age, fifty percent of people—yes, that is one in two people—have or have had a mental illness. The economic burden of mental illness is estimated at $51 billion per year in Canada with the cost of a disability leave for mental illness about double the cost of a leave due to a physical illness. Serious mental illness costs America $193 billion in lost earnings per year.

With labour costs already consuming the lion's share of annual municipal tax revenue, ensuring the physical and psychological safety of civic employees is critical for sustainable service delivery and community well-being.

In short, our citizenry and circumstances are just not the same as in previous decades. We are left facing the same question posed by Socrates some 2,500 years ago, namely, "What is the point in battleships and city walls, unless the people building them and protected by them are happy?"

PART TWO

JOURNEY
TO SUSTAINAVILLE

3
·····

SANCTUARY

Such places exist among the endless abodes of every major city, places that seem to be sanctuaries from the present, immune to the hustle and bustle, the sound and fury that in the end change nothing. Like long unopened books sitting upon dusty shelves, there exist people filled with knowledge that has somehow been saved from extinction. But buried as they are by time, there abides in them yet a seed awaiting the proper condition for germination. There is some process that occurs in dormancy, some subtle shifting of the fabric of reality that science has yet to discover. From such forgotten places as these occasionally springs, in some unseen future, a gigantic oak whose day has come.

—James Rozoff, *Seven Stones*

*As long as there is one upright man, as long as there is one
compassionate woman, the contagion may spread and the
scene is not desolate. Hope is the thing that is left to us, in
a bad time.*

—E.B. White, Letter to Mr. Nadeau, 1973

Every year, a virtual city springs up in the wilds of interior British Columbia. The citizens are festival goers, artists, merchants, medical personnel, employees, and volunteers. At fifteen thousand people, it is larger than any municipality within hours of driving in either direction. It's called Shambhala, an electronic music festival, now in its twenty-first year.

As the city manager in a neighbouring municipality, I worked with festival organizers as you would with any regular municipality, to establish protocols in the case of an emergency, backup water supply, fire services support, and other such things. For an administrator, the complexity of the undertaking was impossible not to appreciate. Even though the festival is only one week long, there still must be water and sewer infrastructure, medical services, food services, waste management, facilities for bathing, security services, and human resources—all on top of the logistics and creative challenges of putting on a good show.

Overall, it was a very impressive feat. But what really struck me on my first tour of the festival was an enclosed area, like a massive tree fort nestled in a grove of old growth trees, with a big sign in front of it carved in wood. THE SANCTUARY.

It was not really part of the tour, but I just had to go in. The festival organizers were sophisticated in mass gatherings and had all of the medical facilities to deal with emergencies as well as a special safe space for women; this place, however, was unique to that and open to all.

> *The Sanctuary is a calm safe haven nestled in a grove of old growth trees right next to Medical Services. The Sanctuary provides non-judgmental service and support and welcomes anyone who feels they need a safe, quiet place to rest at any time during the festival. If you are feeling stressed, overwhelmed, isolated, cold, wet, need to get out of the sun for a while, just need to chill out, or need someone to talk to, our Sanctuary volunteers will be happy to help. Sanctuary is open 24 hours a day.*[17]

I wanted to stay there for a while. A long while, if possible. The tour guide in her woodland-fairly-like costume could have waited all day. But my guests could not. So we moved on, but the value of establishing such spaces in communities everywhere has never left me.

REFUGE FROM THE STORM

It's interesting that the practice of offering sanctuary comes to us from medieval Europe. Perhaps there is a natural law that dictates that, where there is great darkness, there must also be great light. Sanctuary was extended to keep even accused felons safe and fed for up to forty days, often while mercy or pardon was sought or exile arranged. According to literary scholar and professor at the University of California, Elizabeth Allen, offering sanctuary in medieval England, which she studies, had a symbolic value that "marked people's vulnerability and made protecting them a sacred duty" as well as a moral duty and legal obligation "enshrined in both canon law (law of the church) and secular common law."[18]

This is the same principle, namely the principle of equality expressed as *all men are created equal and worthy before God,* like a divine seed planted in the heart of humanity, that Tocqueville describes as the driving belief behind the "great democratic revolution". In his trip to the continent, he expressed scorn for the injustice of slavery and the extortion and dislocation of the aboriginal peoples. These were examples that betrayed democracy and could threaten its very existence.

Today, sanctuary is most commonly associated with offering support and protection for refugees whom the state seeks to deport. Some US cities distinguish themselves as "sanctuary cities" or *not* "sanctuary cities" depending on whether they will cooperate with federal immigration law enforcement officials. The Canadian Sanctuary Network supports the practice of providing sanctuary to refugees and describes this age-old practice as grounded in an affirmation of faith "that human life is sacred and worthy of protection."[19]

During the civil rights movement, some churches provided sanctuary for civil rights activists. The bombing of the

Sixteenth Street Baptist Church in Birmingham, Alabama on September 15, 1963, where four young girls were blown to pieces in the church basement by a bomb planted by the Ku Klux Klan, exposed the violence of racist hatred and shattered the sense that there was any place safe, if you were a black American citizen.

> *Rescue workers found a seven-foot pyramid of bricks where once the girls' bathroom stood. On top was a child's white lace choir robe. A civil defense captain lifted the hem of the robe. "Oh, my God," he cried. "Don't look!" Beneath lay the mangled body of a Negro girl.*
>
> *...The remains [of the four girls] were covered with shrouds and carried out to waiting ambulances. A youth rushed forward, lifted a sheet, and wailed: "This is my sister! My God—she's dead!"*
>
> *...[A] Negro minister added his pleas, "Go home and pray for the men who did this evil deed," he said. "We must have love in our hearts for these men." But a Negro boy screamed, "We give love—and we get this!"*
>
> *...Later Negro youths began stoning passing white cars. The police ordered them to stop. One boy, Johnny Robinson, 16, ran, and a cop killed him with a blast of buckshot. That made five dead and 17 injured in the bomb blast.*
>
> —*Time* magazine, September 27, 1963

Hatred, once unleashed, clearly knows no bounds. Had the ministers and leaders of the civil rights movement—who would be clearly justified in their hatred—not called for *love* in return for *hate* many more would have been killed.

The Tree of Life synagogue massacre in Pittsburgh, motivated by racist hatred towards Jews, happened on the Sabbath, October 27, 2018. They were gathered to worship as well as welcome a new baby boy into the world, when the gunman opened fire killing eleven people in the sanctuary.

We remember what Canadian police describe as a "barbaric" massacre at a mosque in Quebec on Sunday, January 29, 2017, where people were gathered to pray. Six people were killed and three times as many people were injured by the young gunman.

Today, the places we can consider *safe* are growing smaller in number. The individualism, materialism, envy, and ill will that Tocqueville warned us of has its tentacles woven throughout our cultural fabric.

Canadian author Paul Born, who describes community culture on a spectrum, warns of the rise of fear-based communities[20] where some believe that:

- We have a greater right to life and happiness than they do.
- We are stronger when they are weaker.
- We are right, and they are wrong.
- If we work together, we can win, and they will lose.

These are the hallmarks of divided communities, descending into animosity, incivility, and worse and further away from any sense of social unity based on the well-being of all.

Previously safe places, like schools, can no longer be assumed to be so. In July 2018, the Canadian Teachers Federation released a Pan-Canadian Research Review survey results reporting that violence ranged from forty-one percent to ninety percent among surveyed teachers in jurisdictions across Canada.[21] And we are all too aware of the rise of deadly violence. In May 2018, CNN reported that since 2009, there have been 288 shootings in US schools, averaging one shooting a week in 2018 alone.[22]

The needs of at-risk populations, namely those with mental illness, sickness, addiction, homelessness, and poverty, for safe havens are daily and pressing. While there are many activists and politicians taking bold action in this area, they are too often met with oppositional rage and a lack of compassion or concern. In some cases even death threats arise for attempting to address this human problem in "my neighbourhood".

The old adage "My home is my sanctuary" is further away from realization than it has ever been before. Jane Jacobs states that families and households have been stretched so thin through relentless economic and social pressures that this vital social institution is strained to effectively serve its traditional nurturing function. Social media, video games, and general addiction to screen time has only further undermined family life. Addiction expert and author Dr. Gabor Mate writes in *How to Build a Culture of Good Health* that:

> *Parents stressed by multigenerational trauma, relationship issues, economic insecurity, maternal depression, or social disconnection are simply unable to give their children the "mutually responsive" attuned interactions that optimal childhood development requires. The result is the epidemic of developmental disorders among our children that we are now witnessing.*
>
> *On the societal level, we must understand that health is not an individual outcome, but arises from social cohesion, community ties, and mutual support...We need a broad attitudinal and practical shift, consciously willed and created, toward a culture based on the fundamental sociality of human beings. We know all too well, from data too persuasive and too somber to be disputed, that emotional isolation kills.*[23]

Recognizing this social need, psychotherapist Traci Ruble started Sidewalk Talks, a community listening project in San Francisco, California, in 2015. According to Ruble, the program now has a thousand volunteers in twenty-nine US cities and is active in ten countries. Volunteers sit in chairs on sidewalks, with an open chair before them and an invitation for anyone to sit down and talk. She says it isn't a professional counseling service—they are simply offering "human connection."

Offering sanctuary is a revolutionary act; it expresses love, when others offer scorn or hate. It recognizes humanity, when others deny and seek to debase it. Sanctuary says *we* rather than I. It is belonging—the building block of community.

Sanctuary offers hope that, together, we can expand that sanctuary to all.

NIGHT VISION

There is no question these are dark times. It sometimes takes the calmness and stillness of the night to sharpen our focus, reflect, and ultimately see more clearly the nature of the challenge before us, glimpses of the way forward and our part in it. Martin Luther King Jr. said it best: "Only when it is dark enough, can you see the stars."[24]

The Apostle Paul reminds us that it was God who said, "Let light shine out of darkness" and in so doing "made His light shine in our hearts" (2 Corinthians 4:6). Perhaps these are the *seeds of goodness* that the secular author E.B. White describes as harboured in people, "lain for a long time waiting to sprout when the conditions are right."[25]

In reality, the darkness has always been with us too. We have just been so busy vilifying whomever we perceived to be our enemy we couldn't see it. The enemy could be women, it could be people of a different colour, it could be your neighbour, it could be a person of a different political party or religion, it could be your boss or co-worker, and it could be orphans like in Lemony Snicket's *The Vile Village*. It could be anyone for goodness sake!

And it is this cultural and moral darkness that, if not lifted, this time by us all, poses an existential threat as real as climate change. Because without addressing how we live together and finding a way that respects both nature and our universal humanity, we won't have the collective ability, strength, or shared vision necessary to protect our world or build a better one.

A new study published in the *Journal of Positive Psychology* examined the psychological and social implications of holding a "notion that everything that exists is part of some fundamental entity, substance, or process." As expected, they found that people do differ in the degree to which they believe in this "oneness of all." Those who did, whether secular or religious, had greater compassion for people and held values that included a universal concern for the welfare of others. They also felt more connected to others, without sacrificing their sense of personal identity.[26]

This indicates that the individualism versus collectivism narrative is a false dichotomy. That there is a healthy individuality, an independence of mind and thought, that coexists well with concepts of social unity and collaborative action.

This is important, because self-interested *individualism*—the value championed above all others in our modern democracy—is precisely the habit of the heart that Tocqueville warned us could be the undoing of democracy. It's the door through which his dreaded tyranny comes in, namely, when citizens are satisfied that *might is right* so long as it is in the majority. It is the tyranny that turns a blind eye to injustice, sometimes injustice to entire groups of people in our communities such as the homeless, people of colour or women, because the majority declared it to be so. This is the *my-gang-versus-your-gang* divisiveness we see everywhere in politics today.

Tocqueville considers the pursuit of self-interested *individualism* as misguided because the idea that any of us is truly self-sufficient ignores all of the compounded efforts of others who made and make our lives possible. It also has the potential to erode other important civic virtues—like love of one's neighbour and selflessness in the service of others—that make living well together possible.

LONG SHADOWS

You see but your shadow when you turn your back to the sun.

Khalil Gibran, *Sand and Foam*

Perhaps this social and moral responsibility to each other has become harder for us to understand nowadays because we no longer need to erect city walls to stake our territory. City walls are visible reminders that we belong to each other, that we are a community and that we are responsible for each other. They are no guarantees that all will be well within the walls, but they do make it easier to hold leaders, neighbours, and each other responsible. The well-being, or lack thereof, of the community is more apparent to visitors, for instance, when the city is enclosed by walls. Whereas today, we drive past the homeless at a street corner and barely think about where Social Services or City Hall may be, or the homeless shelter (which is likely tucked out of sight). And even if we were to locate these centers of political and moral authority, it is still not clear what community of people is responsible for the care of those who cannot care for themselves.

There were people, however, who inhabited our land before we got here who knew how to live and care for all life within their communities. Indigenous peoples didn't need walls or borders to define their responsibilities to each other, their neighbours, nature, and the earth. They knew the oneness of all, as well as the importance of cultivating the individuality and character of each member. In the words of Ohiyesa, a poet and spiritual leader of the Sioux nation in the late 1800s:

> *Our children were trained in the natural way—they kept in close contact with the natural world. In this way, they found themselves and became conscious of their relationship to all life. The spiritual world was real to them, and the splendor of life stood out above all else... We conceived of the art of teaching as, first and foremost, the development of personality; and we considered the fundamentals of education to be love of the Great Mystery, love of nature, and love of people and country.*[27]

Ohiyesa was four years old when, on the day after Christmas in 1862, the US Government, in Mankato, Minnesota, performed the greatest mass execution in the nation's history, killing thirty-eight Sioux men, while more than a thousand others including women and children were captured and taken away.

We thought our democracy was so sophisticated, but we lacked the character to live out the equality and freedom of all that is at its heart. We couldn't even hear its heartbeat when it was modeled back to us in the halls of democracy with civility and clarity that rivaled Roman Senators in the case of Chief Red Jacket of Seneca, recorded in his famous address on religious freedoms to the US Senate in 1805.

Though the tragically aggrieved party, the Chief's address was filled with references to the white man as "friend and brother" and wisdom that sought unity, respect, and well wishes for all. When Chief Red Jacket concluded his address, he rose and approached the missionary responsible for evangelizing to his people and extended his hand.

The missionary, it is recorded, refused to take it.

We are so surprised at the incivility and injustice we are experiencing today in the political sphere, trickling down from national politics to local communities. *Trump didn't shake Clinton's hand, so I don't need to shake the hand of the candidate who just unseated me for Mayor.* A contagion of incivility.

Besides, why shake hands when a handshake doesn't mean much today anyway? This too is not new. The history of our relationship with First Nations is one of serial broken promises, handshakes, contracts, and treaties. That's what you do to people when you don't value their humanity.

We are shocked by today's rape culture and blame it on anything from Hollywood to the latest public figure, but we forget that, before there was television, the leadership of the people who settled the continent denied the basic humanity of both those who they enslaved, as well as those who inhabited the land before us. And why?

For the purpose of enriching themselves.

And rape and the destruction of the family and all sense of security were an integral part of the program. The message to people whose humanity is not valued is there is no sanctuary for you here. No place to hide. No place to run.

Then there are the pundits, whose memories must be very short, who posit that the election of Donald Trump as president is the cause of this explosion of incivility and chaos. Yet, we didn't mind when Trump's incivility was entertainment—firing people into oblivion before a national audience. How many employers, fueled by this example, harshly terminated individuals whose value and potential they did not see, when they could have invested in them, or sought their talents or even an agreeable transition? Employees are people who live in communities. Let's stop pretending workplaces are separate from community, places where robots go to die.

Violence, injustice, and incivility pulse like a dark vein throughout Canadian and US history—but so do our democratic ideals, our innovation, and our hope for renewal.

VISIONS OF SUSTAINAVILLE

Visions are important. In the words of George Washington Carver, Black slave turned decorated botanist and inventor, "Where there is no vision, there is no hope." To inspire and direct our footsteps, visions must come from the heart—which is why so many corporate vision statements remain as inanimate as the paper they are drafted on.

When they come to us in the night, visions are called dreams. The very movement of history seems to be directed by the conception of these dreams and efforts to realize them. How we conceive of the future, in other words, is of utmost importance to our collective destiny.

In the rubble of the collapse of Western Rome in the fifth century, Saint Augustine of Hippo envisioned *The City of God*, a colossal book, a thousand pages in Latin alone. This book is considered by many to be the most influential book in medieval Europe.

In 1678, John Bunyan, the English writer and Puritan preacher shared his vision of a journey from the City of Destruction to the Celestial City, written from his jail cell where he was imprisoned for conducting worship outside the walls of the established church. *The Pilgrim's Progress: From This World to That Which Is to Come* is a one-hundred-thousand-word journey that includes being saved from the false promise of Mr. Legality and his son Civility in the City of Morality—by which he conclusively rejects law without heart and order without justice.

About one hundred years later...

Puritan thought was instrumental in the early development of the colonies and in the public acceptance of the US Constitution and Declaration of Independence. Founding Father George Washington was not only the first president of the United States, but he was also the first to use the biblical metaphor of the Promised Land in 1785 to describe this new democratic nation.

About one hundred years later...

In a heart-wrenching two-hour speech in 1879 before an assembly of congressmen and dignitaries in Lincoln Hall, Washington, DC, Nez Perez Chief Joseph pled the case of his people who were defeated, sick, and dying on a reservation in Kansas—no place close to home. He committed to showing his heart and sharing his people's dream, tragically unrealized though practically identical in meaning to those of the founding fathers:

Treat all men alike. Give them the same law. Give them all an even chance to live and grow. All men were made by the same Great Spirit Chief. They are all brothers. The earth is the mother of all people, and all people should have equal rights upon it. [28]

He shared, however, that his father, "[who] had sharper eyes than the rest of our people," could see through the "schemes" earlier than others and warned his people against trading with those who are untrustworthy or who seemed "anxious to make money."

About one hundred years later...

Just like Chief Joseph, Martin Luther King Jr. came to Washington, DC, and in his famous 1963 "I Have a Dream" speech, attempted to collect on this *promissory note* contained in the nation's founding documents. The one that guaranteed the unalienable rights of life, liberty, and the pursuit of happiness to all. His dream included living in a place where there existed a genuine brotherhood of man; a place where the promises of democracy were made real; a place where people were not, through poverty and discrimination, cast as exiles in their own land.

Perhaps it was Tocqueville's *providential fact* that moved Martin Luther King Jr. to encourage the march for freedom forward until it "rang from every village and every hamlet, from every state and every city."[29]

And we don't have to go to a rally or read a book to share these visions and these dreams. We need only to look into our hearts—into the habits of our hearts—and perceive those values we hold and those actions we engage in, both individually and collectively, that clearly do not align with those dreams.

This has everything to do with the way we treat each other—the ones we love as well as those we may call enemies, our neighbours, our coworkers, our leaders, those who work for us, people whom we associate with, those with whom we collaborate, and those with whom we disagree.

It has everything to do with the way we educate in our society—from the home to the nursery school, elementary, high school, higher learning, and continuing education.

It has everything to do with how we prepare and encourage people to be active participants—citizens—in their community and our societies.

It has everything to do with the way we govern, manage, and lead our governments, businesses, and organizations.

It has everything to do with the way we steward our assets, be they capital, natural, or human.

It has everything to do with understanding that the way in which we live, produce, and consume puts us on a fatal collision course with the natural world, and finding ways to do this differently, and sustainably.

But it will all be directed by our emerging collective vision of Sustainaville. Not only do we need to formulate and articulate this sustainable future vision together, but we also need to embrace it in our hearts—as we all have our share, our duty, in its manifestation.

The most widely accepted vision or definition of our sustainable future is a community that is "economically, environmentally and socially healthy and resilient"[30] with "development that meets the needs of the present without compromising the ability of future generations to meet their own needs."[31]

Sustainaville, this vision of the Promised Land, is one we can achieve. And we will decide as citizens, communities, and nations, through unity of action and a sense of collective purpose, whether we will wander for forty years through the wilderness, distracted by endless quarreling, as we circle the same mountains over and over again—or take the direct route, which if followed with clarity of purpose, requires no more than a few days on foot.

The direct route is one where everyone—not just some sustainability experts, environmental gurus, or government departments—understands our purpose, our values, ways to live them, and how to measure progress holistically.

While it is good to celebrate success, how we define success is important. We have become all too aware of how the traditional GDP (gross domestic product) is a poor measure. It says little about human well-being, especially in countries characterized by great inequality and disparity of opportunity. It says nothing about the sustainability of the way we live within the environment.

We have all sorts of awards that celebrate important innovations in what is being called the Fourth Industrial Revolution. This is a new digital age, where data and smart technology are disrupting economies and industries and attracting world investors to erect brand new megacities in places such as India, Egypt, and Morocco that are green and smart-wired before they are inhabited by a single citizen.

Or will they be citizens? What is their governance structure? Is it a democracy? Who ensures justice? What privacy laws and enforcement mechanisms exist to restrict the misuse of data collected by everything from smart sidewalks to storefront windows?

If new technologies and innovation were the comprehensive answer to our sustainability challenges, Palo Alto in Silicon Valley may well be our model. The city hosts the headquarters of so many of the world's major high-tech companies from Tesla to Skype—companies cities everywhere compete to attract. It has consistently ranked in the top GDP per capita or "richest city" scales and has a highly educated population and high employment numbers.

And yet...

Palo Alto is now being dubbed the suicide capital of the US with a disturbing trend of "cluster suicides" taking place among teenagers. The youth suicide rate is almost three times the nation's national rate.

If achieving 100% renewable energy was enough of a goal, the mountainous African country of Lesotho would be our model. Through a major utility asset project, called the Highlands Project—a network of dams that exports water to South Africa providing almost all of the country's power along the way—it has met this mark.

The project, however, is rife with controversy, including serious corruption.

If the gospel of urban transformation was enough, if healthy built environmental planning was sufficient, then we would be modeling our communities on the town of Celebration in Florida. This master-planned community was built by the Disney Corporation in 1991 to be a utopia, a place where everything is perfect, and people are happy, happy, happy.

The reality in Celebration is that the residents—91% white and 1.5% black—report the creepy and eerie feeling of living in what residents call "the bubble" and the social isolation that results from stepping outside of it in any way. It is neither inclusive nor diverse nor happy.

Over the course of my consulting work, I responded to a request for proposal from a First Nations community that was seeking a firm to draft their *Sustainability Charter*, the type of document that many municipalities are now incorporating in their planning in one way or another (either through their own volition or because it is becoming a prerequisite for accessing grant funds from higher orders of government).

While we have been struggling to learn how to think holistically about environment, the economy, and the well-being of society, this document began by explaining that the new terminology we are using to describe sustainability is "built into the history and values of our peoples."

The task, then, was to describe, in our modern terms, what they already knew—but our hearts could not hear.

May our hearts hear this time, that the path to Sustainaville, to be lasting and effective, is people, planet, and prosperity—powered by a sustainable ethos or culture as the engine that sustains us.

For those who still despair at the great sustainable community-building task before us, remember the words of the brilliant Israeli politician and diplomat Abba Eban: "Men and nations behave wisely when they have exhausted all other resources."[32]

4
·····

JOIN THE RENAISSANCE

The society that loses its grip on the past is in danger, for it produces men who know nothing but the present, and who are not aware that life had been, and could be, different from what it is.

—Aristotle

We need a renaissance of wonder. We need to renew, in our hearts and in our souls, the deathless dream, the eternal poetry, the perennial sense that life is a miracle and magic.

—E. Merrill Root

Danny Bowman was fifteen when he first started posting selfies to Facebook. A handsome blond-haired young Adonis, he was an aspiring model and, understandably, found enormous validation and confidence from the positive comments and "likes" of his Facebook friends.

But then came the criticisms—one said his nose was too big for his face, another found fault with his skin. Danny set off on a mission to capture and post the perfect selfie, one that would elicit a validation high and not the pain of criticism and rejection.

It reached a point where he would spend ten hours a day, taking up to 200 photos of himself on his iPhone. Eventually, he shunned all human connection. He dropped out of school, remained housebound for half a year, lost his friends, became belligerent towards his parents if they tried to intervene, and lost twenty-eight pounds in his attempt to capture the perfect self-portrait.

On the days Danny couldn't capture the perfect selfie, he started popping pills. On one particularly bad selfie day, he tried to commit suicide. Luckily his mother found him and rushed him to the hospital where he began his long journey to both physical and mental recovery.

Today, Danny has become an educator on the addictive nature of technology and an advocate for those who suffer from technology-related mental illness. He says, "People don't realize when they post a picture of themselves on Facebook or Twitter it can so quickly spiral out of control. It becomes a mission to get approval and it can destroy anyone."[33]

Sean Parker, an early investor in Facebook and now "conscientious objector" says such social media sites are designed to exploit what he calls a "vulnerability in human psychology" that addicts the user and consumes vast amounts of their time.[34] This vulnerability has been around since the beginning of time. It's a shame that we, the users of social media, didn't immediately recognize the danger.

The ancient Greeks knew about this vulnerability and even had a superstition about staring at one's reflection for too long, a superstition represented in myth. Parents taught their children the story of Narcissus, the handsome hunter who knelt by a lake to quench his thirst, saw his attractive reflection in the water, and couldn't drink or leave the spot for fear of losing sight of it. Eventually, he died of love and thirst, and out of the ashes grew a narcissus flower.

The lesson here was that self-obsession, whether motivated by self-love or self-loathing, leads us to lose all affection for others and wither into nothingness. We have either forgotten or are refusing to heed this warning today.

Rather, our culture seems to encourage, harness, and even *cultivate* self-obsession, most tragically by indulging our youth, against the wise warnings of the ancient Greeks. The authors of *The Narcissism Epidemic: Living in the Age of Entitlement*[35] chronicle the obsession that our modern culture has with the self—the dramatic rise in plastic surgery, the elaborate birthday and prom demands of teens, ordinary people hiring paparazzi to follow them around so they look famous, high school students physically attacking a classmate and posting it on social media to revel in their victory, and the all-too-common impulse to live beyond one's means in order to appear richer than one is.

Yesterday's antidote to narcissism—human connection, self-denial, and sacrifice for others—works just as well today. These cultural characteristics not only foster a healthy self-image, but also contribute to what makes communities healthy, strong, and vibrant.

LOOKING BACK AND LEAPING FORWARD

It is tempting indeed to look at today's complex community-building challenges and focus all our attention on innovation and technology. After all, the possibilities seem endless and the capabilities formidable.

But are these innovations actually solving our problems or merely mitigating them—and thus in a way even abetting them? Are we looking for workarounds to make our current behaviour somehow viable when what we ought to be doing is looking to address and fundamentally change those aspects of our behaviour that aren't?

For instance, according to the October 2018 McKinsey & Company *Public Sector* report, cities are now being offered digital or "smart" solutions such as real-time crime mapping, using statistical analysis to highlight patterns; predictive policing, anticipating crime to head off incidents before they occur; sensor-equipped asthma inhalers, providing data that allow cities to map poor-quality air locations and address them; and sensors on existing infrastructure systems, alerting civic works crews of problems before there is a breakdown and improving service delivery by avoiding interruptions.

In fact, a general flourishing of ideas, skills, and solutions in technology, innovation, economic policy, and healthy-built environment planning is exactly what we need to address the formidable sustainable community-building task before us.

However, this flourishing will only lead to Sustainaville—a place where human well-being is the ultimate measure—if we collectively ensure that this creative explosion meets and serves the needs of residents and citizens. Egypt, for instance, is building a new capital "smart" city with all the bells and whistles. Commissioned by the current president who overthrew the country's first democratically elected president, the construction is being bankrolled by the people. And the new city's governance structure? The army will manage and control the whole city via the command and control centre which analysts say is there to insulate the government from the threat of popular uprisings. Not exactly the Promised Land.

The last march out of a Dark Age was the great cultural revolution known as the Renaissance, French for *rebirth*. Just like today, the people of medieval Europe had forgotten their roots—disconnected from the past, they knew little about the great civilizations that had preceded them, the political philosophy that informed them, the science of architecture and infrastructure, or even the stories of the ancient ruins upon which medieval cities were built.

In Florence, Italy, in 1462, a young Lorenzo de Medici, after a lifetime of being groomed for leadership, was at the helm. His family was prosperous, in great part, because of the bank they owned. A man of his times, he was inspired by this turn to classical antiquity to find lessons that could be applied to inform the way people lived and built magnificent cities.

The family bankrolled the early Renaissance, hiring people to track down ancient Greek and Roman manuscripts in the monasteries, courts, and libraries of Europe; to build the Medici library of classical works; and to put the ancient ideas into practice in every form of cultural expression from the arts, to city design, to architecture.

Those in the employ of Medici uncovered and applied ancient ideas. In architecture, for instance, these ideas told them that the well-being of a people is influenced by the buildings around them. Today, we consider this to be a new discovery—it's called an *emerging field*. Roman historian and politician Sallust further argued that the public square must be well constructed and maintained to invoke the pride of all and provide a space where communal life is promoted.

Great artists like Michelangelo, Botticelli, Leonardo da Vinci, and Raphael were commissioned to produce magnificent works of art to inspire and direct this cultural revolution by expressing classical values of beauty, truth, and wisdom. There was an unprecedented openness to humanist thought exemplified in the now infamous painting by Raphael in the

Vatican, *The School of Athens* featuring Plato and Aristotle at its centre.

In 1440, the German printer Gutenberg introduced the printing press, and the written ideas of classical antiquity flooded Western Europe, guaranteeing the furthering of this cultural revival.

The Renaissance was also responsible for reawakening, in the heart of the people, the dream of democracy which is still alive today.

Unlike our modern consumer society, political philosophy and ideas of governance were paramount to the ancient Greek and Roman mindset. The concepts of the *just society* and the *good life* preoccupied them. So too did ideas such as citizenship, citizen engagement, and participation. Topics such as ways to mitigate against abuses of power and ways to secure community well-being were often and openly debated in society—debates that involved politicians, philosophers, students, lawmakers, military men, poets, and the general citizenry.

And this rich Western democratic community-building tradition—which is our own and a gift to us—was born from a struggle against extreme poverty, tyranny, injustice, instability, and war, and enormous experimentation with varying municipal political orders and in-depth observation and analysis of the costs and benefits of each.

And it bore fruit.

In 507 BC, the ordinary citizens of Athens led a revolution that led to the first democratic city-state.

Today we speak of enormous challenges and change. Can you imagine being a political leader, administrator, or active citizen of any one of the hundreds of city-states or municipalities in Ancient Greece?

You have the volatility of an undiversified economy (primarily agrarian) set against continual battles between tyrannical rule and populist pressures for justice and democracy. In Athens, for instance, the people cried out for written laws rather than oral laws because the aristocrats would manipulate and alter oral laws at will for their own benefit.

Around 620 BC, the Athenian ruler Draco enacted what are known as the first written laws. Allegedly written in blood, they prescribed the death penalty for almost all crimes, including the theft of an olive. It is from Draco that the word draconian derives.

Historically, this was still considered an advancement because it enacted the *rule of law*, which is a necessary precursor to civil society, democracy, and stable governments. Today, even countries like India are still struggling to establish a single unified rule of law across the country, for there are still vast areas where *citizen justice* or alternative local rules dominate, and there is no capacity for uniform law enforcement.

I like to look on the bright side of things—though things are tough for us, at least we don't have to worry that a neighbouring municipality will invade, enslave, and slaughter our people.

Instead, cities often collaborate with each other either directly or through regional, provincial, and national associations as well as shared communities of practice.

But isn't this a new era, with entirely new realities? What did ancient Greeks and Romans know about social media, blockchain, climate change, and green infrastructure?

LESSONS FROM CLASSICAL ANTIQUITY

American–Canadian author and urbanist Jane Jacobs was in her late eighties when her book *Dark Age Ahead* was published. In it, she argues that cities are on the verge of cultural collapse. In a live book interview, she is asked the obvious question: *what is to be done?*

The elderly Jacobs leaned over, lifted her eyebrows, and said something to this effect: "*Do the right thing. In the end, it's much easier than doing the wrong thing.*"

She further advises that we should not seek solutions to complex problems in ideology, which may prevent us from seeing possibilities or only accept solutions that fit neatly within a particular belief system. Rather, seek solutions based on evidence, including anecdotal, rational, and independent thought and effective action.

And just like in the last Renaissance, Jacobs argues that cities—their leaders and their people—are the main line of defence between cultural decay and cultural revival. This is because when cities have effective governance, active and collaborative civic associations, and civil society with a healthy culture, they are capable of resolving problems and meeting citizen needs most effectively.

Let's apply classical thought to modern-day sustainable community-building challenges to help us more clearly define what doing the right thing is.

Greek philosopher Aristotle contends that everything has a function and that "the good" can be found in the fulfillment of that function, purpose, or end (Gr. *telos*). The role or purpose of a dwelling, then, is to provide a place to live. The purpose of a clock is to keep time. But what is the purpose of local government?

Local Government 101 today teaches that there are two schools of thought on the role of local government. The first is to provide goods and services such as streets, water supply, sewage disposal, and bylaw enforcement, among others.

The second is that the role of local government is to foster community well-being through democratic local government, citizen engagement, and building a sense of community and prosperity. This was the view espoused by Aristotle. Namely, civil society and the democratic city-state exist to ensure the human flourishing (Gr. *eudamonia*) of its citizens, who are wired by nature to live in community.

In reality, these are not competing schools of thought. Rather, one describes *why* local government exists (namely, to foster community well-being). The other describes *what* local government does to achieve the why (namely, deliver public services to meet community needs).

There has been a recent revival of this teleological thinking in the work of thought leader and author Simon Sinek. In his wildly popular TED Talk[36] and book *Start with Why*, he has shown individuals, organizations, and businesses that purpose-driven activity is effective activity. The key, then, to effective community building action—government or community-driven—is knowing your *why*.

LOCAL GOVERNMENT GOLDEN CIRCLE

Inspired by Simon Sinek

WHAT?
Sustainable Service Delivery

HOW?
Good Governance &
Asset Management

WHY?
Community Well-Being
(Economic, Social, Environmental)

kalenconsulting.com

There are many local governments and community groups that think they have a governance problem for which they need a governance expert; or a volunteer recruitment problem for which they need a public relations expert; or a retention problem for which they need a human resources professional; or a compliance problem for which they need a lawyer—when in fact, they have a *why* problem. They have forgotten their ultimate purpose and, therefore, find it impossible to foster the type of unity and consistency of action required to carry out their work effectively.

In most jurisdictions, legislation governing municipliaties binds them to fulfilling the above purposes—why and what—and makes clear that this comes with a duty to "provide for good government" and "stewardship of the public assets" of your community. These duties address the *how*, and the way to fulfill them is through (1) good governance and (2) asset management.

GOOD GOVERNANCE IS SUSTAINABLE

Good governance is the art of putting wise thought into prudent action in a way that advances the well-being of those governed. In the context of local government, good governance involves the responsible stewarding of all assets—capital, natural, and human—to ensure sustainable service delivery to citizens.

But how do you know if your local government is delivering services sustainably? That's where asset management comes in. It's not just another modern buzzword. Rather, asset management has been around since people began building public infrastructure. The Romans, for instance, built and maintained dams, and provided water, sewer, and garbage collection services to its citizens. They constructed more than 85,000 kilometres of roads and over 200 aqueducts, some of which still carry water today. Now that is sustainable service delivery!

This does beg the question: Why don't we build infrastructure to last much longer than fifty to seventy-five years? It's great that we are now seeing the value of natural assets and using nature to defend against flooding. However, we would not be here at the end of an infrastructure lifecycle if we thought longer term, sooner.

Today, our governance and operational prowess are such that it is possible—as it so happened in a municipality in rural Saskatchewan this year—that a brand-new bridge for vehicular traffic collapsed only six hours after the grand opening. Thankfully no one was hurt, but the short-sightedness of the explanation for this catastrophic infrastructure failure is telling. Representatives said they thought it was too expensive to do a geotechnical report.

Clearly, classical antiquity has something to teach us when it comes to sustainability, governance, and asset management.

In his *Meditations*, the great Roman Emperor and philosopher Marcus Aurelius recalls what he admired most about his adopted father and mentor, Emperor Antoninus Pius, who like Marcus, was remembered as one of the Five Great Emperors of Rome:

> *"[My father's] constant devotion to the empire's needs. His stewardship of the treasury. His willingness to take responsibility—and blame—for both.... The way he kept*

public investments within reasonable bounds—building projects, festivals, distributions of money, and so on— because he looked into what needed doing and not the credit to be gained from it."[37]

Antonius Pius sounds like a great asset manager. His public legacy reinforces this. He was known as a just and effective administrator, leaving his successors a large surplus in the treasury, all while expanding water infrastructure across the Empire, ensuring access to drinking water for all citizens, and for conferring citizenship rights to freed slaves.

You can check off almost every principle of good governance right there—responsive, equitable, inclusive, effective, efficient, accountable, and the list goes on.

The leadership character qualities that Antoninus was known for were **clemency (compassion)**, **dutifulness**, **intelligence**, and **purity**. His adopted son Marcus didn't fall far from the apple tree. Even Machiavelli—who recommended criminal virtue (calculated criminal acts that can help one get ahead in politics) to his medieval masters—openly admitted that Marcus Aurelius governed masterfully as a **lover of justice**, **a hater of cruelty**, and that he was **sympathetic** and **kind**.

Why do these leadership character qualities and core values matter? They matter because good governance in a democracy is impossible without fostering, in our communities and the electorate, an appetite for leaders who are committed to respectful conduct. And without good governance, council and boards cannot effectively fulfill their duty to promote the social, economic, and environmental well-being of the community.

When a community culture is unhealthy or uncivil—as it is in the rising fear-based communities described by Born—neighbours fear neighbours. As a result, anti-bullying municipal bylaws have been cropping up across US and Canadian municipalities as a way to protect people today against rising incivility. In some cities, the laws hold parents legally responsible for bullying done by their kids. Neighbours can be fined for engaging in social isolation, name-calling, taunts, online bullying, and emotional abuse—with penalties for those who either aid or are complicit in the bullying. However, we all know a legislated solution to a cultural problem is only a band aid and not a solution.

Similarly, workplace anti-bullying and harassment laws have been reinforced in both the US and Canada, with psychological harassment now beginning to be taken as seriously as physical violence in the workplace. While this is helping to protect people today, municipal workplaces with toxic cultures are mired in costly third-party investigations and grievance proceedings that not only cost precious tax dollars, but ultimately also affect service delivery.

State and provincial bodies representing municipalities have been considering various ways to address the problem of uncivil conduct at the council table. Some have opted for integrity commissioners to investigate and enforce respectful conduct, others for codes of conduct that include a commitment to a set of core values for respectful conduct.

Besides eroding public trust and creating costly organizational paralysis, toxic behaviour points to a deeper cultural problem that is the collective responsibility of civil society—community leaders *and* citizens—to intentionally address. The disproportionate impact municipal leaders have on the culture at city hall and in the community (through influence and cumulative impact) puts increased responsibility on local government to set an example and be an agent of positive culture change. A similar increased responsibility rests on the shoulders of community and business leaders.

Culture, whether it be organizational or community, is like a forest. The seeds are your core values. Once they take root as behaviours, they can grow into trees, populating your cultural forest. Bad seeds produce unhealthy forests, infertile, and plagued by infestations. Good seeds produce a healthy forest and ecosystems that support life. One is sustainable, the other is simply not.

A RETURN TO THE ART OF LIVING WELL TOGETHER

For a community to be whole and healthy, it must be based on people's love and concern for each other.

—Millard Fuller, *Founder, Habitat for Humanity*

In the ancient Greek mindset, it was impossible to divorce ethics from politics. Since humans are social animals, the study of politics is how we act in relation to each other—what they called the "art of living well together."

It was Plato's belief that the values of society mirror the values of the individual. And further, that the city is a reflection of its citizens. The core values that philosophers of his time felt were integral to good governance and community well-being were practical wisdom, self-control, social courage, and justice.

To advance the development of these values and characteristics in the citizenry and community leaders, Plato established the Western world's first university—the Academy—for the character development and ethical training (e.g., logic, reason, discernment, wisdom, etc.) of citizens to ensure the flourishing of society into one that is just and fosters community well-being.

This was also the original mission of the new world universities like Harvard, whose charge was "to instill in their students piety, loyalty, and responsible citizenship" and were "more concerned with the character development than the unearthing of new knowledge."[38] It's not that knowledge was not valued, but there was a belief that acquiring knowledge without wisdom would result in poor use of that knowledge. Modern universities have largely abrogated this mission, replacing it with an emphasis on credentialism, leaving a void in civic education that municipal leaders must seek to fill if we are going to foster a healthy democratic culture.

When establishing organizational core values, consider what is required in implementing council or board policy. Asset management, for instance, is now a must for all municipalities. Operationalizing asset management requires the fostering of an interdependent collaborative culture rather than a reactive one and one imbued with personal responsibility and a strong public servant ethos. To this end, a municipality on British Columbia's Vancouver Island—the City of Courtenay—formulated the following values: *people matter, depend on each other, make a difference, be accountable, pursue excellence, and celebrate success.*

Culture change efforts, to be effective and lasting, will require the development of a change-management plan or road map. We are creatures of habit, and without new values and behaviours being aligned and lived out in both policy and action, toxic culture may just be the thing that stops a council, administration, or organization dead in its community-building tracks.

5
.....

ONE SHIP, ONE DESTINY

The Destiny of Man is to unite, not to divide. If you keep on dividing you end up as a collection of monkeys throwing nuts at each other out of separate trees.

—T.H. White, *The Once and Future King*

If you want to build a ship, don't herd people together to collect wood and don't assign them tasks and work, but rather teach them to long for the endless immensity of the sea.

—Antoine de Saint-Exupery, *Citadelle*

Crabs have a troubling social characteristic that resembles the worst of human behaviour in communities. It is a characteristic discovered by crab fishermen who used to store caught crabs in barrels. They found that if you put one crab in the barrel, the barrel needed a lid to stop the crab from crawling out and escaping. However, put in more than one crab and no crabs would ever get out and a lid was not needed. Why?

They found that though any crab has the ability to crawl out of the barrel, if one crab tries to escape in the presence of other crabs, they will claw away at the crab to bring it down. If the crab doesn't come down, they will gang up on it and claw at it until they cut off its legs/claws and ultimately kill it, if need be, to prevent it from escaping.

The crab-barrel mentality is summed up in this way: "If I can't have it, neither can you."

Sound familiar? Humans don't always behave this way; however, where a culture is toxic—fueled by envy, fear and mistrust—there is a lot more clawing going on. It's the ideal social environment for schemers but deadly to dreamers.

Captain Alain Noel of the *Atlantic Gail*, a crab fishing boat in Shippagan, New Brunswick, says the crab fishing technology today no longer uses barrels. He reminds us, however, in his debonair French accent, that "[the crabs] have claws. For sure they are always working with those claws. One thing we notice is that if they last too long in the pot, they are going to eat each other... they are going to fight and eat each other."

With over twenty-five years of experience as a fisherman from a long line of fishermen, Captain Noel has some fascinating leadership lessons and observations from his seafaring life with his crew mates.

For my ship, we work in a very close area. On a boat, you are stuck. There is no way out besides if the boat is at the dock and you leave the boat. Once we are all on the boat, everybody knows that we are all there and we are there to stay. When we are leaving the port, we are going for four or five days. So, if you start a fight at the wharf when we are leaving, it's going to be a long run.

As a captain, he says he keeps his crew together by keeping everyone focused on their collective purpose and fostering a positive, encouraging, and respectful team environment regardless of the hardships at sea. The culture on commercial ships, he warns us, can be different. He says the larger ships can lack the sense of unity and common purpose that he is able to foster as captain on his smaller ship.

Lots of politics on large boats. I went on a commercial vessel, and it was an entirely different environment. When you are on a smaller fishing vessel, what do you talk about? Fishing.

When you are on a commercial vessel, everything is regulated... Everybody is on the same task and pattern all day long... You know what people do? They talk about each other, destroying each other. That kills me. It's incredible. I was stunned to hear them talking about how that guy is not good, I'm better than him. I didn't like it at all.

On my boat, maybe they talk a little bit sometimes, but nothing compared to a commercial environment. When a job opens up on a commercial vessel, everybody can apply, so everybody talks against each other behind each other's back.

We need leaders like Captain Noel. At forty-three, he figures he's good for another fifteen years. Certainly, Canada's fishing industry and the community he and his crewmates live in are better off for it.

DIVIDED SHIP

The ancient Greeks were aware that "living well together" didn't just happen. That it required conscious effort, civic education, skill, and planning.

You will find in Socrates' parable of the ship, recorded in Book VI of *Plato's Republic*, a rich understanding of the tensions that arise in the democratic city-state as it relates to our basic civic roles and responsibilities.

In his parable, there are three actors on the ship, which represents the democratic municipality. There is:

- the **Captain**, whom we can liken to our council or board representatives
- the **Sailors**, whom we can liken to our citizenry
- the **Navigator**, whom we can liken to our administrators and public servants.

He describes the **Sailors** as "divided against one another" and vying for the attention of the **Captain** whom he refers to as "a little deaf and somewhat short-sighted" and "lacking in complete knowledge of seafaring skills".

The competitive efforts of the **Sailors** are aimed at convincing the **Captain** to hand them power, benefits, or favour for their own personal benefit, and he says they will resort to begging and manipulating the **Captain**, even going so far as to use "mandrake or liquor" to incapacitate the **Captain** in their favour.

To maintain his position, the **Captain** can be easily swayed, against the best interests of the ship, to bow to the interests of constituents allowing them to inadvertently "rule the ship and make use of what's in it" for themselves, their own personal enjoyment, and benefit.

The **Navigator**, on the other hand, stands to the side and keeps his gaze fixed on the sky to monitor the "times and seasons" as well as the "stars and winds". This position requires enormous skill and wisdom—a good navigator must, for instance, be aware of the ship's position at any time, be able to plan the journey (like asset management or strategic planning), be able to estimate both time en route as well as ensuring hazards are avoided or prepared for—such as oncoming storms (like flooding, wildfires, and climate change), rocks or other threats to the ship (risk management).

The way to overcome these incompatible tensions and increase the likelihood that the **Captain** will steer the ship sustainably, is through civic education, which is why Plato considered it "the primary duty of a city state to educate its citizenry"—the **Captain** and **Sailors** included.

In other words, if citizenship rights and a measure of political power—which is true even in a representative democracy—are extended to *the people*, then *the people* have an increased responsibility to be educated in how to manage that power responsibly and to think about the good of all, reflecting on available resources and realities, rather than simply focus on their own immediate benefit or that of their group. Our new social media age has put on display for us just how recklessly and selfishly some citizens are prepared to use this political power.

We see a similar recklessness in the way people vote or threaten to vote. I have heard pundits tell young people who have never voted to "go out and vote," even if they know nothing about the candidates or their platforms, simply go out and "exercise that right." We have all heard residents say or write that a given candidate doesn't have their vote because a particular policy, which was otherwise prudent and in the public interest, didn't materially or positively impact *them*.

Socrates would tell us, don't be shocked.

Unless citizens are trained to think politically and about the common good—current and future—then they will always choose the candy store owner who offers sweets over the medical doctor who offers "bitter syrups and pokes holes in you, cuts your skin and takes your blood" (painful but necessary procedures that promote good health).

It was with this goal in mind that Plato established the Academy. The school had no fees, and the teaching style focused on peer learning; debate aimed at establishing what is good, right, and true; as well as character development. Core curriculum included the cultivation of civic virtues—wisdom, courage, self-governance, and justice—that the ancient Greeks considered indispensable for a well-ordered society.

The trend that pulled us away from looking at local government as an expression of community—essentially a community project—to a corporate business service-delivery model has been damaging. Not only were the titles of public servants changed from things like *city clerk* to *corporate officer* –and– *city manager* to *chief administrative officer*, but also citizens were encouraged to look at local government like a vending machine.

Our collective *why* shifted from fostering social, economic, and community well-being to simply providing civic services.

The vending-machine model is a transactional model that imagines citizens putting their money in with the expectation of a service in return. You don't like the service? You kick the vending machine. Very destructive for all the public servants receiving the kicking, and ineffective when it comes to ensuring the local government serves the *common* good, rather than the diverse demands of competing factions. It is also, of course, divisive by its very nature.

Furthermore, this model casts citizens as passive consumers rather than active and engaged citizens.

Consumers think in terms of their personal self-interest and not the common good. They have no duty or responsibility to create, imagine, or be accountable to (or responsible for) their neighbours or community. They are there to judge, rate, and consume your product. This is a terrible bastardization of the hard-won right to exercise one's right to free speech, assembly, and expression, and the right to vote.

Citizenship, on the other hand, is built not on self-interest but rather on a sense of belonging and shared destiny. It presumes a commitment to the well-being of the community, a responsibility to be informed, act, and speak out when necessary, as well as exercise the right to vote in order to influence the shared destiny of one's community.

To thrive, democracies require such citizens.

If Captain Noel's ship ran according to the vending machine model, the *Atlantic Gail* would be pulled in so many directions the crew would not have the strength to withstand the journey—nor the focus to achieve their quota—and would ultimately arrive back at the dock without meeting their shared goals or their common private goals of bringing home a paycheck to sustain their families and community.

The only way for a ship with a toxic environment to achieve its most narrow productivity (fish catching) goals is through fostering a climate of competition, fear, distrust, and envy. In that way, the sailors will not be happy, but they will, at least, be under control and *might will be right*—or *manipulation will be right*, as is so often the case in such climates. This model, however, belongs to authoritarian regimes and tyrannies.

It does not describe healthy thriving democracies.

According to Plato, only the ship with the wise captain, who respects the expertise and warnings of the wise navigator and engages the sailors in their common destiny, will be a happy community—one where all flourish.

> *Unless . . . philosophers become leaders in the cities or those whom we now call leaders philosophize truly and adequately and there is a conjunction of political power and philosophy . . . there can be no cessation of evils . . . for cities nor, I think, for humanity.*[39]

In other words, only wise thinkers are capable of rising above their narrow self-interest to see and act in the best interests of the community. The goal, then, is to have as many wise thinkers on the ship as possible.

PHILOSOPHER CONSULTANT

Throughout my working years in both the private and public sectors, I have often marveled at how swiftly and efficiently organizations push aside wise counsel and actively seek either internal or third-party affirmation for decisions and actions that wouldn't stand up to the most basic scrutiny and may very well lead to their organization's atrophy or demise.

This is a leadership problem. But it is also a cultural problem. The cultural emphasis—in our modern democratic society—on getting ahead, minimizing personal risk while maximizing personal benefit, and seeing all human relations and commitment to people and organizations as *transactional*, encourages self-centred and self-serving thinking that leads to siloed and/or fragmented action that undermines the common or organizational good.

It's the same thinking that makes it increasingly difficult for: organizations to sustain the execution of a long-term vision; community associations to recruit volunteers; organizational leaders to foster loyalty; unions to foster genuine solidarity among members; and academics, politicians, community leaders, citizens, and students to express controversial ideas.

This is the same misguided individualism Tocqueville spoke of, only made worse by the social habit of staying silent in the face of any controversy—or even injustice—that may negatively affect your present or future commercial interests, whether it be a job, trade, or social prestige.

As innocent, and even noble, as narrowly pursuing your own self-interest may sound in a market economy, over time, it leads to toxic workplaces, organizations, and communities. The reason for this is that a sort of unstable *Jell-O culture* takes form, one where meaningful and lasting human connections—the kinds that form the vital building block of community and is key to human well-being—are continuously shaken or broken.

Sometimes this occurs in big tectonic upheavals, other times in an ongoing series of unsettling tremors. Human connection is based on trust, and it is trust that is continually violated when people do not practice setting aside their narrow self-interests in consideration of the needs and interests of others, such as their coworkers, family, neighbours, and community.

This is what makes Tocqueville's leadership shine so bright. His grandfather was killed by French revolutionaries, and his father only narrowly escaped the same fate. He had plenty of personal reasons to hate the democratic revolution. His narrow self-interest would have been to shore up the *ancient régime* and do everything in his power to spread negative propaganda about democracy and fight tooth and nail to preserve the privileges of his aristocratic class. He set that aside to do his part in history and contribute to the promotion of democracy in Europe, hopefully learning and applying the best from his reports from America. That's wisdom. It's also the result of a lifetime of education on matters of justice and leadership.

There is, however, an encouraging trend in society today; businesses have begun hiring philosophers, and there is talk of large corporations seeking "chief philosopher officers" and "philosophers in residence". Professor Roger Steare is one such philosopher in residence at the Cass School of Business. He told the *Guardian,* in March of 2018, that the assumption that philosophy and profits are incompatible is wrong. Rather, he says that the tension is "between deep wisdom and short-term profit maximization, instead of long-term sustainable value creation."[40]

So, wise thinking and decision-making lead to sustainable action, the very definition of good governance.

City College of New York philosophy professor Lou Marinoff told *CBC radio* that "most CEOs understand that a virtuous organization is actually more functional, and therefore potentially more profitable, than a vicious one."[41] The same is true for local governments.

Marinoff says that in our litigious society, leaders tend to call a lawyer when they are wondering what the *right thing* to do is. Philosophers encourage leaders to think through the moral dimensions of their actions and make more "virtue-oriented" decisions. Marinoff adds,

> *A society that can find use for its philosophers is going to be more productive, creative, and happy.*[42]

And indeed, the management consultants of ancient Greece and Rome were philosophers. Every leader had a philosopher. Alexander the Great's was Aristotle. The citizens of Athens had access to the philosophers of the city through the public academy.

Sounds funny, but that's because our image of philosophers today is so different. We think of philosophers as folks, likely professors, preoccupied with esoteric, theoretical matters and lacking in "street" or practical knowledge.

However, the esteem in which we hold scientific research today, and the credibility we attribute to it, is more or less analogous to the esteem and credibility that philosophy earned in the ancient world. It was the "objective" way that people made sense of the world, i.e., based on facts, evidence, logic, reason, and a study and understanding of nature (biology, physics, zoology), and of course, this included *human* nature (politics, ethics, psychology). In fact, it was the Greeks who distinguished these fields of study from one another.

What we, today, consider *philosophy* was their metaphysics.

What we, today, consider *politics* was their study of *ethics* or *moral philosophy*—the study of goodness, right and wrong conduct, wisdom, beauty, justice, and virtue.

It's instructional that *ethics* was impossible to divorce from the study of *politics*. In their view, man is a political/social animal, and therefore, the study of politics is how we act in relation to each other, in other words, the "art of living well together."

Doing *good* is relational.

You can't be *good* or *virtuous* in the abstract. Or to put it another way, you can do something that looks *good* in the abstract, but if it doesn't improve the well-being of your community or fulfill its rightful function, then it is not in fact good. Rather, it *could* be a social evil.

An example would be a legacy project that seems good on the surface, but if it comes at the cost of the proper management and investment in vital infrastructure—such as the sustainable service delivery of water services—then it is a social evil., regardless of who wins the election.

The word philosophy derives from the Greek roots *philo* [lover of] and *sophia* [wisdom]. These lovers of wisdom were specialists in fostering—both in themselves and in others—what they call *phronesis* [practical wisdom].

Such wisdom requires the development of the *ethical skill* to discern what the right thing to do is in the context of the goal. In the case of community building, to promote *eudamonia* [human flourishing] as well as the *moral skill* or *character* to actually achieve it.

And what do you know? That is exactly what management consultants will tell you today—that it is this alignment of thought and action that forms the basis of thriving cultures.

As such, asset management champions and practitioners would, for instance, be considered to have *phronesis* [practical wisdom] in the stewardship of public assets.

This ethical development, however, was not just for formal *leaders*, but also for *citizens*—since it was a democracy. If citizens hold a measure of political power, then they ought also to have understanding, wisdom, critical thinking skills, and the strength of character to choose or make decisions that promote this community as well-being.

In 387 BC, in order to establish this common cultural foundation for good governance, Plato opened the Academy for the citizens of Athens, where Aristotle studied for twenty years before establishing his own university called the Lyceum.

CIVIC EDUCATION FOR ALL

If, after the preservation of life and property and order, there be one duty greater than another that devolves on any Government, it is the general education of the people... Unless the youth of a country, who cannot be provided with a proper education by their relatives, be provided for by society, what can be expected by a harvest of ignorant, immoral, and irreligious beings?

—The Pocket, *Ottawa Daily Citizen*, Sept 5, 1846, page 2.

The civic training afforded an Athenian citizen was akin to the training given to an athlete or sports team. It involved intense, regular, ongoing, and multidisciplinary, involving exhaustive peer-to-peer learning and mentoring and the development of critical thinking skills through debate and political discourse.

And the goal was to cultivate in the people an appetite for good governance and meaningful community engagement. This training focused on the development of the moral character of citizens through the development of civic virtues that empowered them to be assets to civil society, as well as to their family and friends. Community members were supposed to use their particular talents—whether it be teaching, poetry, or craftmanship—to lift up their fellow citizens and, by so doing, contribute to the well-being of the entire community.

Plato felt that, without this training, people would simply pursue their own ends; they would admire and seek to emulate the outward success of athletes or aristocrats, rather than the prudent counsel of wise leaders; and ultimately, they would be unfit for citizenship or self-government. Citizens would act based on simple opinion, which he considered the lowest form of human knowledge because it requires "no knowledge and no understanding."

Today, the toxic nature of public discourse and lack of social unity on the things we hold in common seem to reaffirm this ancient belief in the role—and indeed necessity—of civic education in the development of a healthy and flourishing democracy and civil society.

Our investment in the development of a healthy civil society is integral to good governance and sustainable community building. The investment, in turn, helps to shape the character of its citizens. As Aristotle points out, "man, when perfected [by civil society], is the best of animals; but, when separated from law and justice, he is the worst of all."

Civic education also helps citizens ensure that democratic institutions remain free—both governments and associations—like societies and trade unions. Tocqueville warned us that the democratic habits of the heart and ethos that enable citizens to exercise these democratic rights include the ability to think critically and act prudently and often courageously. These are skills, like civility, that are taught and not inherited.

And democracy is not—at any level—merely a series of civic mechanisms that operate, on the vending machine model. It is an active community project that must be continuously reproduced and activated by citizens engaging in civil society.

The Renaissance saw the resurrection of the ancient academies in Europe and then in the New World. In 1636, Harvard University was founded with a clear social and political mission to train the world's civic leadership. As stated previously, these new world colleges and universities were "more concerned with character development than the unearthing of new knowledge," which parallels, exactly, the ancient Greek view that wisdom is superior to any knowledge, which can be more easily acquired and doesn't necessarily require virtue. Knowledge on its own cannot be properly applied to any purpose, and because good cannot exist in the abstract, wisdom is needed to put knowledge to good use.

Canada had its own version of these new world universities. A quarter century ago, I attended one of these remnants—Trinity College at the University of Toronto. I was a most unlikely student, from a working-class background who had only attended public school rather than the elite private schools that had supplied so many of my classmates.

It was an utter culture shock for me to arrive at a place so committed to developing community leaders. First, they handed you your academic gowns, which you had to wear around the college—in fact, you wouldn't be served dinner in the dining hall without them—and in peer learning settings such as the vibrant debating and literary discussion sessions.

Then you learned the school songs, in Latin and ancient Greek, which established your mandate to be *Salterre* [the salt of the earth]. The first time we had to recite that "we were the salt of the earth," I thought I had fallen into the hands of an elitist cult. Later I came to understand that, in the ancient world, salt was not just a substance that added flavour to food, but it was the main means of refrigeration. Salt's primary function was to prevent decay. Applied to society, that would be directing your education and efforts to prevent cultural decay.

The leaders of the college would remind us of those who came before—a who's who of Canadian political and business leaders from Ed Broadbent, to the late Ted Rogers and John Labatt, Michael Ignatieff, Adrienne Clarkson, Michael Wilson, the current Mayor of Toronto John Tory, and the list goes on. Even former Canadian Prime Minister Stephen Harper was a student for a short while. The diverse political opinions of the student body were respectfully shared through the development of skills in public discourse and inquiry. New and different ideas were fascinating and useful to refine our own—not viewed as a challenge or a threat that must be annihilated, as political difference is so often treated today.

The libraries were filled with the textbooks of earlier graduates. One such text was the *Student Manual of Ethics*, written in 1907, which reminds you of your duty to society. It has chapters titled things like: The Duties, The Virtues, Character & Conduct, and the Significance of Moral Judgement. In the chapter entitled "The Social Unity" with the subtitle "Self-Realization Through Self-Sacrifice", it has some remarkable instructions for students:

> *We can realize the true self only by realizing social ends. In order to do this we must negate the merely individual self, which as we have indicated, is not the true self. We must realize ourselves by sacrificing ourselves. The more fully we so realize ourselves, the more do we reach a universal point of view – i.e. a point of view from which our own private good is no more to us than the good of anyone else.*[43]

I could not believe what I was reading. That was the 1990s, and society was awash in individualism and self-centered ambition. This instruction sounded like some sort of religious or socialist manifesto, when in fact, it was the instruction to the intended community leaders of a nascent capitalist country that was democratic.

Today, civic education—when it is offered at all—is most often little more than a technical explanation of the orders of government, perhaps going so far as to explore how laws are made and an emphasis on the importance of voting. When this shallow knowledge is combined with our social media age, we have a phenomenon called the "voter selfie" or vanity voting where national news outlets like CNN are compelled, in the public interest, to run syndicated stories on the rules around ballot selfies in every state in the nation.[44]

The need to revive civic education in our modern democracies is of the utmost importance to our future ability to preserve our democratic institutions and civil society. It is critical to preserving the equality of fundamental rights of all people. It is critical to developing the capacity for effective action to address the many complex social, political, economic, and environmental challenges arrayed before us. It is critical if we are going to successfully navigate the Fourth Industrial Revolution, and ensure it truly results in positive disruptions that work in the interests of the people by democratizing social, financial, and political edifices—rather than simply intensifying the concentration of wealth, power, and influence.

The Greeks understood the need for civic education, the Romans understood this, the Renaissance thinkers understood this, and more to the point, the founders of both Canada and the United States understood this.

The First Nations people understood this as well. Ohiyesa, the great spokesman of the Sioux peoples describes the tradition of the Sioux peoples in the preparation and education of their young for a "life of service":

> *Every child, from the first days of learning, is a public servant in training... The birth would be announced by the tribal herald, accompanied by a distribution of presents to the old and needy. The same thing would occur when*

the child took its first step, spoke its first word, had its ears pierced, shot his first game... At such feasts the parents often gave so generously to the needy that they almost impoverished themselves, thereby setting an example to the child of self-denial for the public good. In this way, children were shown that big-heartedness, generosity, courage, and self-denial are the qualifications of a public servant, and from the cradle we sought to follow this ideal.[45]

Part of this renaissance of sustainable community-building includes seeking and incorporating the wisdom, values, and teachings of the world's rich diversity of peoples and traditions. If we seek it, we will find this wisdom all around us.

SUSTAINABLE CULTURE

6
.....

GLOBAL CALL FOR
VALUES EDUCATION

*I'm convinced that if we are to get on the right side of the
world revolution, we as a nation must undergo a radical
revolution of values. We must rapidly begin the shift from
a thing-oriented society to a person-oriented society. When
machines and computers, profit motives and property rights
are considered more important than people, the giant
triplets of racism, militarism and economic exploitation
are incapable of being conquered.*

— Dr. Martin Luther King, Jr.
Speech at Riverside Church, April 4, 1967

In December 2017, Paramount released *Downsizing*, a
clever science-fiction comedy-drama by American director Alexander Payne. The main character is played by Matt

Damon, who together with his screen wife tries to escape their sense, as ordinary working Americans, that they can't ever really get ahead, realize their ambitions, or find happiness. Their restlessness is reminiscent of the "strange melancholy" that Tocqueville observed in the citizens of democratic America—unhappy in the midst of liberty and abundance.

The technology of the day allows them to do exactly that—escape to a land of milk and honey called Leisureland where their small savings are worth millions and promise them all the riches and amenities their hearts could desire. This technology, allegedly designed to save the planet, allows humans to undergo a procedure to permanently shrink or *downsize* themselves to five inches in height, reducing both their figurative and literal footprint on the planet. Of course, while the ecological benefit to a resource-stressed planet is obvious, this is not the true selling point of the procedure.

Instead, it is the prospect of being able, rather ironically, to "live large" on what meagre resources you've already managed to amass in the full-sized world you are choosing to leave behind. In other words, for those who choose the procedure, it has nothing to do with (as one of the characters so aptly puts it) "…all that crap about saving the planet." Instead, "downsizing is about saving yourself. You can live like kings."

And live largely they do—but they also take their habits of the heart with them. The very culture of greed, selfishness, and shallow human connection that make life so unhappy in the first place. Predictably, the social and economic ills such as extreme inequality, exploitation of the poor, indifference to the suffering of others, and unequal opportunity are replicated in this new world.

Payne—also a two-time Academy Award–winning screenwriter—seems to be drawing out the absurdity of a trend we see today. One where we are prepared to do just about anything to address climate change—embrace technology, innovation, even shrink ourselves—so long as it doesn't interfere with our rampant culture of consumption and avarice that has precipitated the crisis in the first place.

The real problem that the downsizing technology is masking rather than addressing—indeed the one it effectively capitalizes upon—is the desire to live like kings in the first place.

Just like in the movie, today's popular culture is one that encourages you to "save yourself" *in spite of* your city, your community, your neighbours, your family, and your friends. This is incompatible with sustainable living, sustainable community building, and a sustainable future.

There is, however, a downsized character called Ngoc Lan Tran that points us to another, more sustainable way. She is a political activist jailed, downsized against her will, and exiled to the slums of Leisureland by her country because she stood up for her Village, which was being flooded and annihilated against their will for a megaproject. She chooses love, caring, and compassionate service to those around her and in so doing, leads those close to her to a more purposeful, meaningful, and ultimately happy life.

THE NEED TO BE INTENTIONAL ABOUT CULTURE CHANGE

Culture doesn't just change because it ought to. It changes because we decide to honestly assess the values, behaviours, and systems that are not working for us—not helping us thrive and flourish as a community—and replace them with ones that do.

The evidence that our culture and the way in which we live is making us sick, is overwhelming—from the epidemic rates of depression, mental illness, addiction, and suicide to the rising anger, divisiveness, and toxic behaviour in the public square.

Sociologists now have a term for this. It's called toxic socialization, a damaging process that happens to human beings when they are in toxic environments. Social scientists confirm that these toxic environments have now spread, like a cancer, everywhere—in the home, the school, the workplace, and the public square.

Toxic socialization is characterized by physical, psychological, emotional, political, and intellectual violence and abuse. It includes bullying, malicious gossip, social isolation, character assassination, neglect, harassment, discrimination, and other socially abusive behaviour and techniques designed to undermine, demonize, and dehumanize others. It is a process that "fractures attachments, undermines self-esteem, destroys ego boundaries, disables the body's ability to function emotionally, psychologically, and intellectually, and generally undermines the health and human potential of the human victim."[46]

Simply put, toxic socialization kills. It kills the human spirit, tears at bonds of trust and connectedness, destroys the hope and potential of individuals and groups, and leaves in its wake trauma and more toxic environments and communities.

Dr. Mike Sosteric, Associate Professor of Sociology from Athabasca University argues for healthy communities to "stem the growing mental health crisis and suicide epidemic... by changing the way we raise, educate and socialize our children."[47]

Just like so many of the problems facing humanity today, our cities and our communities are the first and most effective line of defence. When it comes to culture, we not only have the wisdom of the ages that told us we were wired for human connection and community, and that man is a sociopolitical animal, but there is an abundance of scientific evidence of this.

Robert Putnam, political scientist and professor of public policy at Harvard University set out in the 1990s to prove what everybody sensed, but no one could conclusively show was happening. Namely, that community was collapsing, and together with it the associations, connections, and shared purpose that made democratic communities work.

In his book *Bowling Alone: The Collapse and Revival of American Community* published in 2000, Putnam's survey showed this was happening at an alarming rate. He urged his readers to take the initiative of educating the next generation about civic virtues, reconnecting with neighbours, as well as increasing civic engagement and participation. The civic virtues he encouraged individuals to cultivate were participation in public life, trustworthiness, and reciprocity.

Since then, the social media age has only further fractured what connections did exist. Some social pockets that may have simply been shallow before, have now turned toxic. The wellness industry has exploded, as people search for relief from the hurt, the loneliness, and the lack of meaningful and lasting connection.

After a 2013 report that half of Yale University undergraduate students sought assistance for mental health, the school launched a course called *Happiness 101: The Science of Well-Being*. The demand was overwhelming. In the 2018 spring semester offering of the course, it was reported that nearly 1,200 students enrolled in the course—a quarter of the student body and the largest reported enrollment for a single class in Yale University's 317-year history.[48]

As a service to society, Yale University—which has an annual student tuition of over $50,000 per student—has now made this course available online to anyone for free. Dr. Laurie Santos, the psychology professor who teaches the course told the *New York Times* that she feels the course, by fostering good habits, such as students showing more gratitude and increasing social connections, is "seeding change in the school's culture."

We now know that over thirteen million people have seen the TED Talk delivered in 2015 by psychiatrist Robert Waldinger: *What Makes a Good Life? Lessons from the Longest Study in Human Happiness.* This unique and astoundingly comprehensive Harvard University study showed that close social connections, and warm and trusting relationships were the greatest determinants of human well-being, longevity, and happiness, not money, power, or fame.

The study also found that loneliness kills. And yet reports show it is only getting worse with rates of loneliness reaching twenty-five to forty-five percent of the population in recent surveys in Canada and the United States. Just this year, the United Kingdom appointed a minister to tackle loneliness.

A 2018 US survey conducted by Entrepreneur of the Year found employed people today derive the greatest sense of "belonging" at home (62%), followed by work (34%), significantly behind is neighborhood (19%), and lastly, places of worship (17%).

What's especially tragic is that we know the modern workplace is no sanctuary. Tales of toxic workplaces abound. And whatever happened to places of worship, these spiritual communities where "love your neighbour" is preached? While most people feel they "belong" at home, it is still disturbing that thirty-eight percent feel they don't.

Until we address the issue of culture intentionally—the culture of division, relentless comparison and competition, scapegoating, demonizing others, jealousy, and malicious gossip that seeks to tear "friends" and neighbours down, rather than build them up—we should expect more of the same. Namely, fear-based toxic cultures where bonds are built on common "enemies", rather than a common purpose to advance the well-being of all.

Culture is not something that happens to us. It's something we make happen.

CHOOSE YOUR VALUES WISELY. YOUR CULTURE DEPENDS ON IT.

A culture can be toxic or nourishing. If we wish to take full responsibility for health in society, we must not only be vigilant guardians of our personal well-being, we must work to change structures, institutions, and ideologies that keep us mired in toxic culture.

—Thom Hartmann

We've established that fostering a sustainable culture requires intentionality. Culture is built on the values that are lived in an environment. We need to choose values that build human connection in our spheres of influence and belonging—home, neighbourhood, workplace, associations, school, or businesses.

What those values look like and the ones you choose to foster and emphasize will vary in time, place, and purpose. The values of a volunteer fire department, for instance, will be different than the values of a seniors' social club. Community values emphasized during times of war and scarcity will be different than during times of peace and prosperity. This is why families, organizations, communities, and local governments need to revisit their values and recommit to them often.

Renaissance cultural leaders focused on truth, beauty, wisdom, and a return to the values of classical antiquity. The ancient Greeks, through their study of ethics, established that a community needs people who possess **practical wisdom** to discern the right course of action; self-governance or **self-control** to ensure you had the ability to direct your actions in accordance with your better judgement; **social courage** to ensure you are capable of sacrificing for others or the common good; and, a sense of **justice**, which requires all of the other skills to carry out.

Leo Tolstoy, the author of *War and Peace*, spent a considerable part of his long and prosperous life in search of a people who had mastered the art of "living well together". He looked at peoples from diverse communities and religions and settled upon the Doukhobors, or "spirit wrestlers" who were being persecuted by the Tsar for their pacifist views. He was so dedicated to preserving their way of life, that he wrote the book *Resurrection*, his last novel, published in 1899 and used the proceeds of the sale of that book to fund the travel and resettlement of almost 8,000 Doukhobors to Canada.

The Doukhobor psalm *Be Devout* is not a biblical text but a sort of values manifesto drafted by their people and hung in homes that prescribes their values and ways of life. In addition to trusting God, the psalm counsels community members to be loving, humble, prudent, temperate and not avaricious, righteous, benevolent, gracious, and forgiving. It also provides some interesting ways or principles of living that help to show respect towards others, and build connection and community.

- Keep more to silence than to talkativeness. When someone is speaking, keep quiet. When someone is addressing you, pay attention.
- To all be affable, to none be a flatterer.
- That which you do not know, do not affirm, nor deny; best of all, enquire;
- In adversity, do not lose hope; in prosperity, do not morally deteriorate.
- Help the poor, if thou canst.
- Be courageous, always willing to labour.
- Serve each and all, as much as you are able to.

In my own province, the 2018 foundational principles or values established by the bodies that represent local governments are designed to address challenges at council and board tables with respectful conduct and to promote good governance. These values are: accountability, respect, integrity, leadership, and collaboration.

Communities or organizations that are facing toxic cultures, asset management, or infrastructure challenges may want to emphasize values like social courage, trust, and stewardship. The choice is yours.

The Council of the City of Victoria in Canada, under the leadership of Mayor Lisa Helps, proactively addressed values and culture after a divisive 2018 election campaign. Their first act as a council was to arrive, through consensus, at a *Declaration of Principles and Values*. In her inaugural address, Mayor Helps stated that the process was designed "in order to create a culture of deep respect, to build the relationships, to do the work and aspire to be our highest selves." The declaration includes:

- Governing with integrity, transparency and an unwavering dedication to public service.
- Welcoming diversity and fostering a spirit of inclusion and equity in everything we do.
- Leading with creativity and courage.
- Deep listening and critical thinking.
- Assuming that everyone is here with good intentions to make the community better.

- Nurturing a culture of continuous learning with each other, staff, and the public.
- Working collaboratively and cooperatively with each other, staff, and the public while welcoming a diversity of opinion and thought.
- Practicing generosity, curiosity, and compassion.
- Being patient, kind, and caring.
- Bringing a spirit of open-mindedness and open-heartedness to all of our work.
- Keeping a sense of humour and light-heartedness with each other.

As for putting these values into practice, Victoria Council's public declaration was a great first start, but they also committed to regularly reviewing and recommitting to them.

"City Hall has a huge role to play as a well-being generator," Mayor Helps shared when we discussed values, culture, and the role of government two months prior to the 2018 election. Though the municipal purpose to promote the well-being of the community is enshrined in legislation in most jurisdictions, it is often overshadowed by the vending machine view of local government as strictly a civic service provider.

We are all culture shapers; however, due to their disproportionate influence, political leaders have an even greater responsibility to lead and foster sustainable culture intentionally, as we are seeing in the capital of British Columbia. If not from our leaders, where else are people hearing and learning about values, particularly civic values today?

THE GLOBAL CALL

There are also some universal values that are being emphasized globally and can serve as a guide to fostering the type of sustainable culture needed to build healthy, vibrant, and inclusive communities.

In March 2018, the Dalai Lama held an international conference called *Reimagining Human Flourishing* that explored the need to integrate compassion and ethics in the teaching of youth worldwide to prepare them for our challenging road ahead.

His Holiness is calling for a **cultural revolution of compassion**—which he carefully distinguishes from empathy. Empathy sees another in pain and says, *wow, that must hurt, I feel for you.* Compassion sees another in pain and does everything in its power to relieve the other person's suffering. It's the same concept as the biblical story of the Good Samaritan.

In modern market economies, this seems impractical. One may say, *I see homeless people every day. If I felt compassion for them all, I'd go bankrupt and still not be able to help them. Besides, that's the government's problem.* The key here is that we are called to do "what is within our power" only, starting within our immediate spheres of influence and finding partners for shared responsibility and assistance.

Compassion requires upstanders, not bystanders. Turning a blind eye or remaining silent in the face of injustice is compliance—no matter how sorry you feel for the target. Repeatedly we hear that upstanders are the key to stopping bullying and harassment, which has now reached epidemic levels in our schools, workplaces, and communities. Shallow expressions of empathy are not what it's going to take to make communities safe places that welcome diversity, celebrate inclusion, and build people up rather than tear them down. What is required is courage and a readiness to sacrifice for what is right. Yes, if you stand up to the bully, there may be some negative consequences for you. If you are not prepared to pay this price, then you will not have the reward of a safe environment for your colleagues, friends, neighbours, and family.

Over two million individuals in the world including hundreds of local governments have endorsed the Charter for Compassion, a document that urges the peoples and religions of the world to embrace the core value of compassion. I asked the Charter's Executive Director, Marilyn Turkovich to define the bystander problem. She said it is rooted in a "desire to be liked", which she describes as an obstacle to be overcome.

> *When people expect or crave to be liked, they have missed a step in their own life. They don't have compassion for themselves. If you are secure within your own self, and you know how to take care of yourself, when the accusations*

> *come against you, where people disagree with you, you can*
> *observe what they are saying and distance yourself from*
> *them… I think this is a helpful practice and principle.*

Understanding the need to educate people on how to live their values, the Charter for Compassion has just launched a ten-week training pilot program called Compassionate Integrity Training in Secular Ethics. It promises to cultivate basic human values as skills for the express purpose of increasing individual, social, and environmental flourishing. Graduates are armed with the ability to "live one's life in accordance with one's values and with a recognition of our common humanity, our basic orientation to kindness, and reciprocity."[49]

The Organization for Economic Cooperation & Development, which has historically focused on poverty reduction and economic development, has reoriented to focus also on a new learning framework with goals to be achieved by 2030. These include teaching empathy, responsibility and self-efficacy, motivation, trust, respect for diversity, human life, and virtue to the next generation.

The stated reason for this emphasis on values is that "technology and advancements will lead to only further disparity and strife" without their application through a more sustainable values-based culture. The expressed hope is that education will reduce the likelihood that people are defeated by the challenges we expect the next generation will face. The framework boldly states:

*Children entering school in 2018 will need to abandon
the notion that resources are limitless and are there to
be exploited; they will need to value common prosperity,
sustainability, and well-being.*[50]

Our schools will obviously have the greatest role in fostering such a values-based culture among young people. However,
there is plenty that can be done to promote sustainable and
capacity-building values at City Hall, in community organizations, businesses. and through citizen engagement and
visioning sessions.

The United Nations Sustainable Development Goal
Number 16 insists that the fostering of compassion and a
strong moral compass is essential to every democratic society
to combat the "injustice and abuse that still run rampant and
tears at the very fabric of civilization". In other words, our
institutions, to be sustainable must be just and strong, but
they cannot be that without fostering values of compassion,
accountability, trust, collaborative leadership, and justice.

Michael Green is one of the economists that created the
Social Progress Index, a standard to rank societies based on
how they meet the needs of citizens and promote well-being.
He applied this measure to all countries to determine what
progress the world's nations were making towards achieving
the Sustainable Development Goals. While only Denmark
was expected to meet the 2030 goals, the world was making
moderate progress in most areas.

One area, however, where countries have been either stagnant or sliding backwards for the past three years are in the areas of individual rights and inclusiveness. Green says they are forecasting even further decline, as negative trends are being seen in the largest countries in the world, including the United States.

The last book Martin Luther King Jr. wrote before his assassination was called *Where Do We Go from Here: Chaos or Community?* It seems, for too long the answer has been chaos, and now we are sliding backwards. His warning rings ever truer and even more urgently today.

> *We are now faced with the fact that tomorrow is today. We are confronted with the fierce urgency of now. In this unfolding conundrum of life and history, there is such a thing as being too late. Procrastination is still the thief of time. Life often leaves us standing bare, naked, and dejected with a lost opportunity... This may well be mankind's last chance to choose between chaos or community.*[51]

Chaos or community; the choice is yours. Choose wisely.

LOVE IS THE GREATEST CIVIC VIRTUE

Imagine this tired old world where love is the way.

When love is the way—unselfish, sacrificial, redemptive.

When love is the way, then no child will go to bed hungry in this world ever again.

When love is the way, we will let justice roll down like a mighty stream and righteousness like an ever-flowing brook.

When love is the way, poverty will become history. When love is the way, the earth will be a sanctuary.

When love is the way, we will lay down our swords and shields, down by the riverside, to study war no more.

When love is the way, there's plenty good room—plenty good room—for all of God's children.

Because when love is the way, we actually treat each other well... like we are actually family.

When love is the way, we know that God is the source of us all, and we are brothers and sisters, children of God.

—Bishop Michael Curry,
Royal wedding sermon, May 2018

Love is something you and I must have. We must have it because our spirit feeds upon it. We must have it because without it we become weak and faint. Without love, our self-esteem weakens. Without it, our courage fails. Without love, we can no longer look out confidently at the world. We turn inward and begin to feed upon our own personalities, and little by little we destroy ourselves. With it we are creative. With it, we march tirelessly. With it, and with it alone, we are able to sacrifice for others.

—Chief Dan George,
Chief of the Tsleil-Waututh Nation

One of the most prestigious and high-ranking jobs in the ancient world was that of cup-bearer to the king. Cup-bearers were chosen for their character qualities such as trustworthiness, wisdom, and courage. It was their job to, at all times guard the top political leader from the ill will of competitors and rivals who might resort to murder by poison to achieve their political ambitions.

A good cup-bearer understood what was at stake. If they failed in their mission, not only would the king lose his life, an empire could be sent into chaos, ruling families could be murdered, and people could be left without protection. It was a job that required political savvy—the ability to detect plots, ill will, and dangers to the king. It also required skilled leadership in the monitoring and management of the sourcing and preparation of royal beverages and the application of methods of poison detection. A cup-bearer was prepared to make the ultimate sacrifice by drinking from the cup prior to serving it to the king.

Nehemiah, cup-bearer to Artaxerxes, King of Persia around 445 BC is one of the most notorious cup-bearers of the ancient world because he was also a city-builder. One day, Nehemiah received word that his Jewish people were in serious trouble—the walls of Jerusalem were broken down and its gates were burned by fire leaving the people exposed and vulnerable.

It is recorded that Nehemiah sat down and wept at the news and then for days mourned, fasted, and prayed. He was in such distress that the king, who had never seen him this way before, noticed his sad disposition while he was serving him wine and asked Nehemiah what was the matter.

Nehemiah expressed his sorrow and love for his people to the king, telling him of the broken walls and burned down gates. The king appreciated Nehemiah's service and loyalty and was so moved by his care for his people that he granted him a leave of absence and permission to return to Judah as governor of the province with a mission to rebuild the city.

He also provided him with Persian building materials to help in the efforts.

Once there, Nehemiah was confronted by enormous and dangerous opposition from both within and without. The life of a change agent is never easy, as there are many people invested in any system, no matter how dysfunctional, and will resist any attempt to change it. No stranger to devious and subversive plots, Nehemiah escaped them all and employed his leadership skills to mobilize the talents and skills of his people to rebuild the wall in a record fifty-two days.

As soon as his work was done rebuilding the city walls, the city's main infrastructure, Nehemiah did not return to the comfort of the King's palace. After all, the king commissioned him to "rebuild the city"—that means the people within it too. He turned his attention to the restoration of the rule of law in Jerusalem and renewing the culture of the people so that the people would have the strength and unity to maintain both their walls and their way of life.

The kind of love Nehemiah, this cup-bearer and city builder was displaying, was what is referred to as agapeic love, or *agape*. This is the highest of seven forms of love in the ancient Greek language. In the context of community, *agape* is the love that is unconditional—seeking the well-being of one's neighbour and community without impartiality and without calculating one's own interests. It sees the intrinsic value, worth, and dignity of every human being and does everything it can to ensure its well-being. It is compassionate, and courageous, and seeks justice for the other. It commits to treating people as they ought to be treated based on their membership in the human family, rather than any other measure, such as how likable or favoured they are—the ultimate public servant ethos.

It is at the heart of the age-old democratic revolution, as Tocqueville calls it—founded on the principle of equality expressed as *all men are created equal and worthy*. It commits us to value, preserve, and uphold the rights, dignity, and well-being of all, including our neighbours, those who are different than us, those with whom we disagree, and those who are not yet born. It is a universal principle, a universal love. It's even the substance of a recent Dalai Lama tweet: "We are all fundamentally the same, and therefore equal. Despite all the characteristics that differentiate us—race, language, religion, gender, wealth and many others—we are all equal in terms of our basic humanity." [52]

In a democracy, we are all trusted cup-bearers to each other, commissioned by our common purpose and citizenship to be city builders and community builders.

It is our collective responsibility to each other to ensure what we drink and serve each other—through every interaction, whether it be on the street, at city hall, or at the board table—a life-bearing cup. That is, one that is nourishing and not toxic. Is it infused with love, compassion, and trust? Or is it infused with fear, selfishness, and control? One leads to community, the other to tyranny.

Democracy gives us citizens a measure of political power. That power comes with a responsibility to foster a culture that makes it possible to live and work well together for the well-being of all.

WHEN WILL WE EVER LEARN?

Reports of incivility in politics, but also in daily life, abound. The level of incivility is also intensifying and escalating from rude remarks and failures to hear alternate views, into more serious cases of bullying and criminal harassment in our communities. Not only is this fostering toxic cultures and environments, but also it is affecting the health and well-being of people and communities.

The seriousness of such bullying is hitting national headlines. In November 2018, a CBC news report titled *Toxic Towns* featured chronic problems with bullying and harassment in Canadian rural communities. Earlier in the year, the tragic case of Robert Duhaime, a municipal grader operator who took his own life after intense bullying highlighted the seriousness of the problem. The Workers Compensation Board investigated and attributed his suicide death to his employment. The world was shocked by the news and raw footage that surfaced out of Abilene, Texas where a father and son shot dead a neighbour on September 1, 2018, over a trash disposal dispute.

While those examples are extreme and fall within the jurisdiction of existing workers or criminal legislation, US and Canadian municipalities have been introducing anti-bullying bylaws for those bullying incidents in communities that happen that are serious, but not criminal. In some jurisdictions, parents are being held responsible for the bullying behaviour of their kids in the playground or online. Workplaces have introduced tightened laws in an attempt to protect employees. Local governments are trying a variety of ways to address toxic behaviour at the council table through codes of conduct, the introduction of integrity commissioners, and increased penalties from suspensions to fines for misconduct. What is being proven to us time and time again, however, is that legislative solutions[53], while important to provide tools for today, don't fix the cultural problem which is giving rise to the toxic behaviour.

Fred Rogers, the Presbyterian pastor turned children's broadcaster of *Mister Rogers' Neighborhood* was very intentional about culture. He invested his life in fostering and modeling values of neighbourliness in children, from good self-esteem, self-control, appreciation for diversity, creativity, imagination, and cooperation on his show which aired first in Canada, then the United States for over thirty years. His view was that neighbourliness and community were grounded in love: "The greatest thing we can do is let people know they are loved and capable of loving".

Rogers was deeply troubled with the commercialized pro-graming that was being put before children and said so in one of the most iconic moments in public media—his May 1, 1969, speech to the US Senate Subcommittee on Communication where he defended public television:

> *And I feel that if we in public television can only make it clear that feelings are mentionable and manageable, we will have done a great service for mental health. I think that it's much more dramatic that two men could be working out their feelings of anger—much more dramatic than showing something of gunfire.*[54]

We now see the anecdotal evidence of these "unmanaged" feelings all around us. This lost skill of being able to manage our emotions and handle conflict in a healthy way, a way that respects the other rather than vilifies them, is at the core of so many of our incivility challenges today.

And now, traditionally quiet and safe neighbourhoods are finding themselves plagued by toxic culture, up to and including heinous hate crimes ranging from vandalism to murder. Many didn't realize that the Tree of Life massacre in Squirrel Hill, Pittsburgh on October 27, 2018, believed to be the deadliest attack on the Jewish community in US history[55], happened just a few streets away from where Mr. Rogers lived—yes, literally in Mister Rogers' neighbourhood.

Soon there may not be any "safe" communities left. No sanctuary. No place to run.

We have heard this warning before. We all should recognize the signs—the rising anger, scapegoating, dehumanizing language, the vilification of groups of people and forms of dissent. About a decade prior to Hitler's ascent to power, German philosopher Martin Buber published his most well-known work, *Ich und Du* (later translated into English as *I and Thou*) where he argues we are relational beings and we experience relationships in one of two ways: (1) *I-It*, a subject-object utilitarian relationship, essentially sociopathic when applied to human relations; or (2) *I-Thou,* a subject-subject mutual and reciprocal relationship. The second, he believes is the only way we should experience each other as human beings—that treating the other as another subject, rather than an object is what humanity requires and deserves.

Radhanath Swami, the acclaimed author, community builder, and spiritual teacher summed up this principle very clearly in a recent talk he delivered: "In an evolved human society, people love people, and use things. But unfortunately, so much in this world, people love things and use people to get them and to keep them. There cannot be inner satisfaction in life in such a state of consciousness."[56]

Swami's call is the same as Buber's call for love. A universal love lived out in the way we see and treat each other, regardless of circumstance or difference, rather simply because we are human. We didn't heed Buber's 1923 call. Instead, the world descended into the unthinkable barbarism of World War Two.

Today may be our last chance to say, "Never again."

CIVILITY FLOWS FROM THE HEART

The causes or triggers of incivility in the face of disagreement seem to come from a lack of skills in healthy debate, productive political discourse, and constructive disagreement. They are also fueled by other factors, such as:

- a feeling that incivility is justified when you have been aggrieved.
- the existence of a toxic culture encouraging others to get their own way through uncivil methods.
- a loss of shared vision or sense that we are in this *alone*, rather than *in this together*.

Handling disagreement well is not something we are born with. That's why parents intervene when laughter between toddlers turns to cries as playing children realize they both want the same toy. We personalize these differences, imagine ourselves losing and the other winning and see no way out or around it.

Gone are the days when many of our schools and universities had vibrant debating societies and related civic education.

Social norms no longer dictate that generosity, sacrifice, and warm-heartedness are necessarily civic virtues. *Getting along* takes the second seat in a world where *getting ahead* is championed above all else.

Our sense of social unity and shared vision is also eroded as economic, social, and political tensions pull at individuals, families, and communities. This is exacerbated as scarcity of traditional jobs, opportunities, housing, and prosperity is closing in on generations that were previously promised the world.

The ensuing sense of injustice can also drive some, through a feeling of righteous indignation, to lash back and hurt the other party as they perceive they were hurt.

This debate has taken on monstrous proportions in the United States where the left and right debate what type of uncivil, threatening acts of criminal harassment and violence are worse than others. When is it okay to accost politicians and their families in restaurants? When is it okay to send pipe bombs to the houses of political representatives? When is it okay to beat up your neighbour because he is a member or representative of an opposing political party? The answer is never.

A government of the people, a democracy, has room for peaceful civil disobedience—a practice that appeals to the humanity and sense of justice of the opposition (not defined as the *enemy*) and insists that we all do, in fact, belong to the "beloved community". Martin Luther King Jr. is its most renown advocate. He describes this method as one that "does not seek to defeat or humiliate the opponent, but to win his friendship and understanding."

It is good to remember this example—the enormous strength and dignity of character it takes to express love in the face of hatred—whenever we are tempted to resort to incivility to achieve our goals.

It's also good to remember that incivility spreads like a contagion. Eventually, even those without legitimate grievances use it as a short cut, using intimidation and bullying to get their way.

In other words, we are either part of the solution or part of the problem.

BE PART OF THE SOLUTION

A sports field without rules and without a referee is chaos—like in Suzanne Collins' *Hunger Games*. No amount of resilience, skill, or mindfulness training will enable a fair person to "play" and achieve team objectives without either being pummeled or resorting to end-focused survivalist methods.

Communities are places where human beings come together to thrive, not simply survive. This means that local governments and organizations must have well-meaning rules and norms of conduct. They must be drafted and adopted in the public interest and must be followed and enforceable.

In modern times we have watered down the term civility to mean simple decorum or politeness. Critics rightfully observe that civility, when defined this way, could stifle healthy democratic debate, which requires politicians and citizens to ask questions and express facts and views that may sometimes make others uncomfortable.

To recover the original meaning of civility as it applies to democratic societies we need to turn back to classical antiquity. In Latin, *civilis* means "pertaining to citizens or civic life"; *civitas* means "city", referring to the city-state or *polis*, citizens bound by law and community; and *civilitas* means "civility", the proper conduct of citizens giving of themselves for the good of the city, the commons.

P.M. Forni, cofounder of the Civility Initiative at Johns Hopkins University provides a modern-day definition based on this ancient conception of civility: "The civil person is someone who cares for his or her community and who looks at others with a benevolent disposition rooted in the belief that their claim to well-being and happiness is as valid as his or her own."[57]

This is in stark contrast to the way relations between citizens, neighbours, and their local government are often characterized today. There is a sense that we owe each other nothing but the expectation that we will seek our own advantage or our own way as a matter of civic virtue; and that what connects us is a little more than the fact that we all pay taxes to receive services. Civility, in this context, makes the absurd demand that we seek our own interests, politely.

This modern view denies the core principle that makes democracy desirable and possible. In aristocracies or oligarchies, for instance, the ruling class is accused of serving its own interests ahead of the interests of the people. A democracy is supposed to prevent that, as *its* ruling class *is* "the people" and in serving itself, it seeks the well-being of all.

Democracy is a system grounded in a universal principle—a sense of justice that says we are all equal in our humanity and before the law, that we are all worthy of dignity, well-being, respect, liberty, and security. Preserving this principle is the very essence of civility. Citizens seek the well-being of their neighbours, their city, and themselves as necessary to the preservation of a democratic way of life. Anything other than that is uncivil.

Back to the sports field….

For your local government, community group or organization to thrive, you need rules and norms that serve the common good. Many have already established core values and vision statements and adopted the basic policy documents—such as codes of conduct, respectful workplace, or bullying and harassment policies. Some municipalities also have integrity commissioners and enforcement mechanisms built into policies aimed at ensuring respectful conduct. If done right, and regularly reviewed, this first step will set you up for success.

The next part is living these values, rules, and norms, i.e., living civility. Here are some basic principles for fostering a civil council or board, organization, or workplace, which will in turn have a positive effect on community culture. As community leaders, you set the tone.

Be civil. Be compassionate. The most immediate thing we can all do to address the growing incivility is conduct ourselves well and in a way that respects the humanity and dignity of all, including those with whom we disagree. That includes employees, volunteers, contractors, family, friends, and neighbours. The time for fractured human relations—the kind, for instance, that care for physical assets, but not human or natural assets—is over. We have sown those seeds and reaped their destructive consequences. Moving forward means doing so sustainably, which is to say holistically and with integrity. We're going to get this wrong sometimes. Forgive and do better next time.

Don't give in to incivility. Be courageous. Just like in the schoolyard if you give in to the bully, they get stronger. And the longer you tolerate it, the bigger the problem gets. Don't accept incivility, and speak up for others when they are its target. Educate bystanders and, reward upstanders.

In organizations, pockets of incivility represent a culture risk that sucks the lifeblood out of your group as it allows behaviours that are not congruent with your organization's values and purpose to erode the overall culture, breeding inconsistency and cynicism. Sustainable culture audits can help you track your stated values against the actions and behaviours of leadership and front-line employees or volunteers.

Form civility circles. Just like incivility, civility too is contagious. In any space where there is a critical mass of individuals behaving in respectful ways and not tolerating incivility, bad behaviour is exposed as the obstructive and destructive tool it really is. Civility circles are safe spaces—sanctuaries—where trust, good will, and collaboration flourish; and scheming and gossip die for lack of oxygen.

Gossip, the simple act of talking negatively behind another person's back when they are not present, is possibly one of the most destructive forms of incivility. It destroys trust, ruins friendships, divides teams, tears apart communities, ruins a sense of safety and belonging, stirs up anger and animosity, and attempts to destroy lives and reputations. Fundamentally, it denies the humanity of the person being gossiped about. And it reveals the gossiper as one not to be trusted. Don't tolerate it.

The ancient Greek word for gossip is *diabolos*, condemning it as slanderous, devilish activity. Say no to *diabolos*. And remember that great stain on the Athenian citizens' soul, the conviction and execution of their greatest philosopher

Socrates arose from gossip. Socrates stood in the Athenian agora to face the charges against him and described his fate thus: "It is not my crimes that will convict me. But instead, rumour, gossip; the fact that by whispering together you will persuade yourselves that I am guilty."

If *civility* and *courage* are not foundational values for your group, workplace, or organization, consider making them so. And make no mistake, values like cunningness, respect through fear, and deception do not lead to human flourishing or community well-being no matter how well-intentioned or how compelling the Machiavellian argument is. The philosophers of classical antiquity knew this. Modern science is now proving it to be true.

A recent article in the *Harvard Business Review* called "How Rudeness Stops People Working Together" reports on study after study showing that incivility fractures teams, destroys collaboration, splinters members' sense of psychological safety, and hampers team effectiveness. It also makes frontline employees less responsive to the needs of those they serve.[58] Instead, foster organizational cultures of compassion and well-being. Focus on complementing each other, rather than competing with each other. To do this, we need to be curious and interested enough to discover peoples' unique gifts and take the time to see how we complement each other.

Google recently did a massive two-year study on team performance which revealed that the highest-performing teams have one thing in common: psychological safety and the resilience that comes with it. Fear and mistrust distort our ability to function, adapt, share, and create.

Psychological safety, on the other hand, allows for moderate risk-taking, speaking your mind, and innovative problem-solving that crosses over silos without worrying that you will be punished for "stepping out of line".

Arrange for training. Civility training is all the rage (so to speak), and it comes in many forms. Human resource departments and consultants offer inclusivity and diversity training, as well as respectful workplace education and conflict resolution. Governance and management consultants offer such training, including skills in public discourse, for councils, boards, and senior managers. There are online modules and resource materials at your local library.

City Halls and community organizations can be transformed into local academies of civility, places where the purposes and principles of democracy are modeled and upheld. They are ideally suited for the type of long-term peer-to-peer learning that makes civic education effective and lasting.

Remember, civility involves teachable, learnable skills. Make the business case, if need be—civility is good for business, good for teams, good for democracy, and worth investing in. Legendary investor and leadership expert Ray Dalio says that "the greatest tragedy of mankind comes from the inability of people to have thoughtful disagreement to find out what's true."[59]

Partner with local schools and colleges to model and promote civility. While most parents advise against it, there are too many kids learning from their parents and adults that civic engagement is screaming, yelling, bullying, and seeking to humiliate elected officials or staff in a public setting, including online. Education leaders do not support or tolerate bullying at school and are your natural partners in sending a strong message to students—the next generation—that bullying is just as unacceptable in the public square as it is in the schoolyard.

Many communities already invite elementary and high school students to visit the local government and learn about what civic services are provided to residents. There are many creative ways to engage students to also learn about governance, civility, cooperation, and civic values.

Love your neighbour. Above all else, civility is about respect for the human dignity and worth of all. It is a declaration that we are connected and that despite our differences, we belong. It is the glue that holds us together and makes constructive dialogue possible. It is the cornerstone of community building. It is *agape*—the unconditional love that treats you right because you are human, not because of anything you did or any advantage to be gained.

In short, civility flows from the heart. And the heart-work must be done by us all.

I leave you with this beautiful true encounter and model civil discourse between India's Minister of the Environment and popular spiritual guru, Radhanath Swami, at an airport a few years ago. Swami was tired after a long pilgrimage and hoping for some quiet rest when he was approached by the minister who expressed her frustration with what she saw as his wasted energy on worship and spiritual matters that could be used to clean the rivers, restore the soil, and save the planet.

Swami shared a parable that likens skin boils to environmental challenges. He started by agreeing that it is true that when boils appear on the body they must be topically treated as they are given time to run their course and heal.

But if the boil comes from an internal blood condition, the underlying cause must also be addressed. Swami saw himself as addressing the underlying cause of all the pollution and damage to the environment, what he called "toxic greed", selfishness, and jealousy by helping to transform them into love, generosity, and joy for each other. He further expressed these thoughts to the Minister:

> *[The cause of pollution] is pollution within the human heart. When our heart is polluted, we are going to, through our words and actions and the decisions we make, we are going*

to pollute the world, because what's inside is expressed by what we do and say. We have to address, we have to educate people on how to live in harmony with themselves, how to live in harmony with each other, how to live in harmony with God, and how to live in harmony with nature.

And today's world now, it has come to a point, with all of our incredible science, our incredible technology, the unbelievable development of industry and the armies and the weapons and the bombs, and the incredible power of communications. If we don't use these things with the right attitude, and the right motives, we have the power to really cause serious destruction...

If we don't clean up the internal state of human consciousness, even if you clean every river, every ocean, all the air, and all the ground, as long as that selfish egoistic greed is there, they are just going to pollute it all over again.[60]

The Minister of Environment listened intently. Swami then described how his work was doing his part to help the environment, while she did her part and urged her to consider working together.

She smiled. "Yes, we must work together".

Let us all work together in love.

APPENDIX

ROADMAP
RENEWING CIVIC CULTURE

Be Civil. Be an Upstander.

Be intentional about culture. Know and live your values. Champion civic values such as compassion, justice, wisdom and courage. Be a transformational servant leader. Stand up for others.

Assess Culture Risk. Measure Well-Being.

We measure what we treasure. Diagnose and measure your culture. Human flourishing is the goal. Pursuit of the common good. Plan accordingly. Culture audits. Culture change management plans.

Form Civility Circles.

Foster safe spaces. Offer sanctuary. Respect and cherish others. Cultivate psychological safety. Be inclusive. Celebrate diversity. Build trust, connection and belonging. Encourage collaboration.

Prioritize Civic Education & Training.

Ongoing, values-based, purpose-driven, servant leadership training. Partner with schools. Lobby for better civic education. Advocate for independent media. City Hall as civic academy. Democracy champions.

Love Your Neighbour.

Golden Rule reflected in person, policy and action. Ethics in human relations. Compassionate community. Inclusive, ongoing civic engagement, community dialogue. Peacemaker. Volunteer.

Download colour poster ➤ **SaveYourCity.ca/newsletter**

©2021 Diane Kalen-Sukra

ACKNOWLEDGMENTS

The people and influences that made this book possible were those that persuaded my heart and my mind that we are built for belonging and for love; and that, to think this, is not to be a dreamer, but a realist about the kind of families, friendships, workplaces, communities, and nations that are possible when we choose to wish and seek for others what we wish and seek for ourselves.

I had the privilege of loving parents, siblings, grandparents and extended family and the warmth and love of life that comes from growing up in a small village, the neighbourhood of Unionville in Markham, Ontario. We were also shaped by the vibrant Greek community on the Danforth in Toronto, where our family had small businesses. In our home, when the kids were allowed to watch television, it was *Little House on the*

Prairie, Mister Rogers' Neighborhood, and *Sesame Street.* I thank both my parents and the programmers of those shows for their positive influence on my idea of civic values and community.

In university, I was blessed by remarkable professors who inspired and proved conclusively the enormous application of political philosophy to daily life—the way in which we decide to live and act as neighbours and citizens in a democracy. We are all eternally indebted to Socrates (as remarked by the Roman orator Cicero) for bringing philosophy down from the heavens and into our homes, cities, and the public square.

In my years in the social justice movement, it was the example of a few courageous souls that stood out for me—their impact reaching far beyond their numbers. A special thank you to retired union representative Timon Azmier for risking all to do what is right. And I will always cherish the memory of my dear friend Bev Lapointe, who is no longer with us. She was someone who never turned a blind eye to injustice and approached community disputes as an opportunity for love and shared understanding. Thank you for your example.

I have been moved and inspired by the remarkable comradery, wisdom, and integrity of my colleagues in the municipal sector. There are too many to name, but I would like to especially distinguish Wally Wells, Executive Director of Asset Management BC who has invested his life crusading for the proper management of public assets. There is a love of community-building that seems to unite local government servant leaders. It is reflected in the positive, enriching, and supportive culture of the body I proudly belong to, the Local Government Management Association.

This book is dedicated to my cherished family, my late husband Jerome and our four children who have not only blessed me every day of my life, but who have blessed every community we have ever lived in through their volunteerism, kindness, and example. Love you infinity and beyond infinity, as Sophia says...

·····

ENDNOTES

1   Coletta, Amanda. "Hate Crimes in Canada Surge 47%,
    Fueled by Attacks on Jewish, Muslim and Black
    Populations." *The Washington Post*, WP Company, 4 Dec. 2018,
    www.washingtonpost.com/world/2018/12/04/hate-crimes-
    canada-surge-fueled-by-attacks-jewish-muslim-black-popula-
    tions/?utm_term=.9ae24835ddb2.

2   "The Relentless Cycle of School Shootings in the
    US." *SBS News*, 18 May 2018, www.sbs.com.au/news/
    the-relentless-cycle-of-school-shootings-in-the-us.

3   Bridges, Alicia. "Toxic Towns: Bullying and Harassment
    Described at Rural Municipalities." *CBCnews*, CBC/
    Radio Canada, 12 Nov. 2018, newsinteractives.cbc.ca/
    longform/toxic-towns-saskatchewan.

4   Cirla, Andrea. "Despotism (Encyclopædia Britannica
    Films, 1946)." *YouTube*, 7 Apr. 2017, www.youtube.com/
    watch?v=Mu150EzIBoI.

5   Smellie, Sarah. "No Need to Vote: Why an Acclaimed Council
    Threatens Local Democracy" *CBCnews*, CBC/Radio Canada, 11
    Sept. 2017, www.cbc.ca/news/canada/newfoundland-labrador/
    more-acclamation-less-democracy-1.4282358.

6   Born, Paul. "New Year's Message." *Paul Born's Blog*, Jan. 2018, deepeningcommunity.ca/blogs/paul-born.

7   Levitsky, Steven. *How Democracies Die*. (Random House USA, 2018).

8   Jacobs, Jane. *Dark Age Ahead*. (Vintage Books, 2005), p. 9

9   Gibb, Ian. "Vanishing City Hall." *The Signal*, University of King's College School of Journalism, 2 Dec. 2018, http://j-source.ca/article/vanishing-city-hall/

10   Tocqueville, Alexis de. "Democracy In America, Book 2, Chapter 13." *Pullman*, xroads.virginia.edu/~hyper/DETOC/ch2_13.htm.

11   Madison, James. "Federalist Papers No. 51 (1788)." *Bill of Rights Institute*, billofrightsinstitute.org/founding-doc-uments/primary-source-documents/the-federalist-papers/federalist-papers-no-51/.

12   Nayna, Mike, director. *Academics Expose Corruption in Grievance Studies. YouTube*, 2 Oct. 2018, www.youtube.com/watch?v=kVk9a5Jcd1k&feature=youtu.be.

13   Kalman, Frank. "Frank Kalman – Talent Management." *Talent Management*, 2010, talentmgt.com/author/frankkalman/.

14   Tocqueville, Alexis de. "Democracy In America, Book 2, Chapter 20." *Pullman*, xroads.virginia.edu/~hyper/DETOC/ch2_20.htm.

15   Gardner, Sue. "Public Broadcasting: Its Past and Its Future." *Knight Foundation*, 2017, knightfoundation.org/public-media-white-paper-2017-gardner.

16   "What Is Civility?" *The Institute for Civility in Government*, 2018, www.instituteforcivility.org/who-we-are/what-is-civility/.

17   "Our Story." *Shambhala Music Festival*, 2018, shambhalamu-sicfestival.com/info/#health-and-safety-services.

18   Allen, Elizabeth. "What's the History of Sanctuary Spaces and Why Do They Matter?" *The Conversation*, 19 Sept. 2018, theconversation.com/whats-the-history-of-sanctuary-spaces-and-why-do-they-matter-69100.

19   "Guidelines for Church Groups and Congregations Considering Sanctuary." *Canadian Sanctuary Network*, sanctuarycanada.ca/?resources%3Aguidelines_for_church_groups_and_congre-gations_considering_sanctuary.

20   Born, Paul. *Deepening Community: Finding Joy Together in
      Chaotic Times*. Berrett-Koehler Publishers, Inc., 2014. p. 62-63

21   Alam, Hina. "Violence in Schools on Increase, Says Report
      by Canadian Teachers Federation." *Edmonton Journal*,
      11 July 2018, edmontonjournal.com/news/local-news/
      violence-in-schools-on-increase-says-report-by-canadian-te-
      achers-federation.

22   Grabow, Chip, and Lisa Rose. "The US Has Had 57 Times as
      Many School Shootings as the Other Major Industrialized
      Nations Combined." *CNN*, Cable News Network, 21 May 2018,
      www.cnn.com/2018/05/21/us/school-shooting-us-versus-world-
      trnd/index.html.

23   Maté, Gabor. "Gabor Maté: How to Build a
      Culture of Good Health." *YES! Magazine*, 6 Aug.
      2018, www.yesmagazine.org/issues/good-health/
      gabor-mate-how-to-build-a-culture-of-good-health-20151116.

24   *King, The Rev Martin Luther. "Martin Luther King's Final
      Speech: 'I've Been to the Mountaintop'—The Full Text."* ABC
      News, *ABC News Network, 3 Apr. 1968,* abcnews.go.com/
      Politics/martin-luther-kings-final-speech-ive-mountaintop-full/
      story?id=18872817.

25   E.B. White to Mr. Nadeau, North Brooklin Maine, March 30,
      1973, in Letters of E.B. White, Edited by Dorothy Lobrana
      Guth. New York: Harper Collins, 2006

26   Kate J. Diebels & Mark R. Leary (2018). The psychological
      implications of believing that everything is one, The Journal of
      Positive Psychology, DOI: 10.1080/17439760.2018.1484939

27   Kent Nerburn, ed., The Wisdom of the Native Americans:
      Including The Soul of an Indian and Other Writings of Ohiyesa
      and the Great Speeches of Red Jacket, Chief Joseph, and Chief
      Seattle (Novato, California: New World Library, 1999), 98.

28   Kent Nerburn, ed., *The Wisdom of the Native Americans:
      Including The Soul of an Indian and Other Writings of Ohiyesa
      and the Great Speeches of Red Jacket, Chief Joseph, and Chief
      Seattle* (Novato, California: New World Library, 1999), 186.

29   "Martin Luther King's I Have a Dream Speech August 28
      1963." *Andrew Carnegie Wealth June 1889 < 1876-1900 <
      Documents < American History From Revolution To Reconstruction
      and Beyond*, www.let.rug.nl/usa/documents/1951-/martin-luther-
      kings-i-have-a-dream-speech-august-28-1963.php.

30   "Definition of Sustainable Community." *Institute for
      Sustainable Communities*, 2018, sustain.org/impact/
      definition-sustainable-community/.

31   "The Brundtland Report 'Our Common Future'." *Sustainable
      Development*, 2015, www.sustainabledevelopment2015.
      org/AdvocacyToolkit/index.php/earth-summit-history/
      historical-documents/92-our-common-future.

32   Trumbull, Robert. "Japan Welcomes Eban Warmly; Her Industry
      Impresses Israeli." *The New York Times*, The New York Times,
      19 Mar. 1967, www.nytimes.com/1967/03/19/archives/japan-wel-
      comes-eban-warmly-her-industry-impresses-israeli.html.

33   Molloy, Antonia. "'Selfie Obsessed' Teenager Danny Bowman
      Suicidal after Failing To." *The Independent*, Independent Digital
      News and Media, 28 Mar. 2014, www.independent.co.uk/news/
      uk/home-news/selfie-obsession-made-teenager-danny-bow-
      man-suicidal-9212421.html.

34   Ong, Thuy. "Sean Parker on Facebook: 'God Only Knows
      What It's Doing to Our Children's Brains'." *The Verge*, The
      Verge, 9 Nov. 2017, www.theverge.com/2017/11/9/16627724/
      sean-parker-facebook-childrens-brains-feedback-loop.

35   Jean M. Twenge and W. Keith Campbell, *The Narcissism
      Epidemic: Living in the Age of Entitlement* (New York: Atria
      Books, 2010)

36   Sinek, Simon. "How Great Leaders Inspire Action."
      TED Talk, TED, September 2009, www.ted.com/talks/
      simon_sinek_how_great_leaders_inspire_action.

37   Marcus Aurelius, *Meditations: A New Translation*, trans.
      Gregory Hays (New York: Modern Library, 2003), 10–11.

38   Suzanne W. Morse, *Renewing Civic Capacity: Preparing College
      Students for Service and Citizenship* (Washington, DC: George
      Washington University, 1989), 27

39   Plato, *Republic* V. 473c11-d6

40   Tickle, Louise, and Claire Burke. "I Work Therefore I Am:
      Why Businesses Are Hiring Philosophers." *The Guardian*,
      Guardian News and Media, 29 Mar. 2018, www.theguardian.
      com/business-to-business/2018/mar/29/i-work-therefore-i-am-
      why-businesses-are-hiring-philosophers.

41   "Why Businesses Are Hiring Philosophers to Help Their
      Bottom Line | CBC Radio." *CBCnews*, CBC/Radio Canada,
      2 Apr. 2018, www.cbc.ca/radio/thecurrent/the-current-for-
      april-2-2018-1.4600420/why-businesses-are-hiring-philoso-
      phers-to-help-their-bottom-line-1.4601980.

42   Ibid.

43   John S. MacKenzie, *A Manual of Ethics* (Toronto: University
      Tutorial Press, 1907), 294

44   Willingham, AJ. "Here's What Each US State Says about Taking
      Ballot Selfies." *CNN*, Cable News Network, 2 Nov. 2018, www.
      cnn.com/2018/11/02/us/taking-selfies-when-voting-laws-in-
      states-trnd/index.html.

45   Kent Nerburn, ed., The Wisdom of the Native Americans:
      Including The Soul of an Indian and Other Writings of Ohiyesa
      and the Great Speeches of Red Jacket, Chief Joseph, and Chief
      Seattle (Novato, California: New World Library, 1999), 103.

46   Sosteric, Dr. Mike. "Toxic Socialization." *The Socjourn*, 16 Mar.
      2016, www.sociology.org/toxic-socialization/.

47   Sosteric, Dr. Mike. "Teen Suicide Is on the
      Rise and This Is Why." *The Conversation*, The
      Conversation, 7 Sept. 2017, theconversation.com/
      teen-suicide-is-on-the-rise-and-this-is-why-83563.

48   Mercado, Mia. "Here's How You Can Take Yale's Famous
      Course On Happiness Online For Free." *Bustle*, 13 Nov. 2018,
      www.bustle.com/p/yales-happiness-101-course-is-available-
      online-for-free-heres-how-you-can-take-it-8706978.

49   *Compassionate Integrity Training*, Life University, 2018,
      www.compassionateintegrity.org/.

50   "Education 2030: The Future of Education and
      Skills." *Organization for Economic Cooperation and
      Development*, 5 Mar. 2018, www.oecd.org/education/2030/
      E2030%20Position%20Paper%20(05.04.2018).pdf.

51   Martin Luther King, Jr., *Where Do We Go From Here:*
     Chaos or Community? (Beacon Press, 2010)

52   Lama, Dalai. "We Are All Fundamentally the
     Same...." Twitter, 5 Oct. 2018, twitter.com/DalaiLama/
     status/1048143485126098944.

53   Yard, Bridget. "Anti-Bullying Bylaws Popular but
     Ineffective in Saskatchewan" *CBC/Radio Canada*,
     13 Nov. 2018, www.cbc.ca/news/canada/saskatoon/
     bullying-bylaw-update-weyburn-1.4902100.

54   Deibler, Daniel. "May 1, 1969: Fred Rogers Testifies before the
     Senate Subcommittee on Communications." *YouTube*, 8 Feb.
     2015, www.youtube.com/watch?v=fKy7ljRr0AA.

55   Ahmed, Saeed. "The Pittsburgh Synagogue Shooting Is Believed
     to Be the Deadliest Attack on Jews in American History, the
     ADL Says." *CNN*, Cable News Network, 28 Oct. 2018, www.cnn.
     com/2018/10/27/us/jewish-hate-crimes-fbi/index.html.

56   Kee, Ong Chin. "The No 1 Mistake We All Make." *YouTube*, 25
     Mar. 2018, www.youtube.com/watch?v=RSGgLv7rHyM.

57   Forni, P.M. "Why Civility Is Necessary for Society's
     Survival." *Dallas News*, 23 July 2010, www.dallasnews.com/
     opinion/commentary/2010/07/23/p.m.-forni-why-civili-
     ty-is-necessary-for-society_s-survival.

58   Porath, Christine. "How Rudeness Stops
     People from Working Together." *Harvard*
     Business Review, 20 Jan. 2017, hbr.org/2017/01/
     how-rudeness-stops-people-from-working-together.

59   Grant, Adam. "Billionaire Ray Dalio Had an Amazing Reaction
     to an Employee Calling Him out on a Mistake." *Business*
     Insider, 2 Feb. 2016, www.businessinsider.com/
     ray-dalio-management-strategy-bridgewater-2016-1.

60   Swami, Radhanath. "Judging Others" *YouTube*,
     ISKCON Desire Tree, 20 Jan. 2015, www.youtube.com/
     watch?time_continue=500&v=-Ky-U91EjYU.

INDEX

A

Agape 144, 159

B

Bullying 14, 15, 22, 48, 55,
    95, 126, 136, 146,
    147, 152, 154, 159

C

Citizen 35, 50, 52, 63, 78, 87,
    88, 90, 113, 138
Citizenship 28, 87, 94, 97,
    104, 106, 114, 145
City 10, 11, 21, 24, 28, 29, 30,
    31, 43, 52, 53, 54, 55,
    56, 59, 60, 69, 70, 73, 74,
    75, 78, 86, 88, 90, 96,
    97, 98, 102, 103, 105,
    110, 125, 133, 134, 138,
    143, 144, 145, 153, 158
City hall 23
Civic values 135, 159, 166

Civic virtues 69, 113, 128, 151
Civil 16, 25, 27, 33, 34, 36, 42,
    45, 51, 52, 62, 63, 88, 89,
    90, 96, 113, 114, 115,
    118, 151, 153, 155, 160
civility 54, 71, 114, 153,
    154, 155, 156, 157,
    158, 159, 160
Climate 15, 21, 25, 48, 53, 68,
    89, 103, 106, 125
Community 10, 12, 13, 14, 16,
    21, 22, 23, 25, 26, 27,
    30, 35, 39, 41, 43, 45, 48,
    50, 52, 54, 56, 64, 66,
    67, 69, 70, 73, 76, 77,
    79, 80, 84, 85, 87, 90, 91,
    92, 95, 96, 97, 98, 102,
    105, 106, 107, 108, 109,
    111, 112, 113, 114, 115,
    119, 125, 126, 127, 128,
    131, 132, 134, 138, 139,
    144, 145, 147, 148, 149,
    151, 153, 154, 155, 157,
    158, 159, 165, 166, 167

Crab 99, 100
Culture 10, 11, 13, 15, 16, 17,
    22, 28, 30, 31, 32, 33, 34,
    35, 42, 43, 50, 51, 54, 64,
    66, 72, 80, 83, 90, 95, 96,
    98, 100, 101, 108, 115,
    121, 124, 125, 126, 127,
    129, 130, 133, 134, 135,
    137, 138, 144, 146, 147,
    148, 150, 155, 156, 167

D

Dalai Lama 135, 145
Democracy 11, 16, 24, 27, 28, 30,
    31, 32, 33, 34, 35, 36, 37,
    42, 46, 47, 49, 51, 62, 68,
    71, 75, 78, 87, 88, 94, 104,
    109, 112, 114, 115, 145,
    146, 151, 154, 158, 166
Democratic 16, 22, 25, 26, 30,
    32, 33, 34, 35, 42, 46,
    51, 62, 73, 74, 87, 88,
    90, 98, 102, 108, 109,
    114, 117, 118, 124, 127,
    138, 145, 153, 154
Dreams 39, 73, 76
Duty 45, 62, 77, 92, 95, 103,
    106, 113, 116

E

Education 14, 16, 26, 42, 48,
    51, 70, 76, 98, 102, 103,
    109, 113, 114, 116, 117,
    118, 137, 150, 158, 159
Ethics 97, 111, 116, 131, 135, 137
Eudamonia 90, 112

F

Fear 10, 15, 27, 47, 64, 83,
    95, 100, 106, 130,
    145, 157, 158
Flourishing 9, 85, 90, 97, 112,
    114, 135, 137, 157

G

Governance 10, 22, 27, 29,
    78, 87, 89, 91, 92, 93,
    94, 97, 110, 112, 113,
    114, 133, 158, 159
Greek 30, 40, 86, 87, 90, 97, 112,
    115, 116, 144, 156, 165
Greece 36, 88, 110

H

Happiness 64, 75, 124,
    128, 129, 153
Harassment 55, 95, 126,
    136, 146, 151, 154
Harvard 27, 97, 115, 127, 157
Heart 30, 35, 36, 42, 62, 68,
    71, 73, 74, 87, 114, 124,
    145, 150, 160, 165

I

Innovation 25, 44, 73, 78,
    84, 85, 125

J

Justice 35, 36, 42, 74, 78,
    88, 94, 97, 109, 111,
    114, 131, 138, 141,
    145, 151, 154, 166

K

Knowledge 59, 97, 102, 110,
    114, 115, 117

L

Love 9, 12, 17, 43, 54, 63, 64, 67,
    69, 70, 76, 83, 96, 126,
    129, 141, 142, 143, 144,
    145, 147, 149, 152, 159,
    160, 161, 165, 166, 167

M

Martin Luther King Jr. 67, 75, 139, 151

N

Neighbour 9, 12, 13, 36, 43, 67, 69, 129, 144, 146, 151, 159

P

Public 10, 13, 15, 21, 23, 24, 25, 27, 29, 30, 31, 35, 38, 42, 50, 51, 52, 53, 54, 72, 74, 84, 86, 90, 91, 92, 94, 96, 98, 102, 104, 105, 107, 110, 112, 114, 115, 116, 118, 119, 126, 127, 128, 134, 145, 148, 152, 158, 159, 166
Purpose 15, 27, 41, 50, 72, 77, 90, 91, 92, 101, 115, 127, 130, 131, 134, 137, 145, 156

R

Radhamath Swami 160
Renaissance 16, 81, 85, 86, 87, 89, 115, 118, 119, 131
Roman 71, 86, 87, 93, 166
  Rome 28, 73, 93, 110

S

Sanctuary 14, 39, 61, 62, 64, 65, 67, 72, 129, 141, 149
Schemes 38, 39, 75
Ship 99, 101, 102, 103, 106, 107
Sustainable 11, 12, 26, 32, 54, 56, 77, 80, 85, 90, 92, 93, 96, 110, 112, 114, 119, 121, 125, 130, 134, 135, 137, 138, 156
  Sustainability 77, 78, 79, 80, 93, 138

T

Tocqueville 30, 32, 33, 34, 35, 36, 37, 39, 46, 62, 64, 68, 69, 75, 108, 109, 114, 124, 145
Toxic 10, 15, 22, 23, 29, 33, 54, 95, 96, 98, 100, 106, 108, 114, 126, 127, 128, 129, 130, 133, 145, 146, 147, 148, 150, 160, 169, 173

U

Uncivil 95, 150, 151, 154
  Incivility 10, 11, 14, 15, 22, 47, 48, 54, 55, 65, 71, 72, 73, 95, 146, 148, 150, 152, 155, 156, 157
United Nations 138

W

Well-being 9, 10, 11, 15, 16, 35, 36, 48, 56, 65, 70, 77, 80, 85, 86, 87, 90, 92, 95, 97, 105, 106, 108, 111, 112, 113, 129, 130, 134, 138, 144, 145, 146, 153, 154, 157
Why 11, 17, 91, 93, 94, 100
Wisdom 9, 11, 12, 14, 16, 30, 71, 86, 97, 103, 109, 111, 112, 115, 119, 127, 131, 142, 166

ABOUT THE AUTHOR

Diane Kalen-Sukra is an author, acclaimed speaker and advisor. Her published works include the books *Save Your City* and *Civic Resilience*, as well as her writing as a national columnist for Municipal World magazine and Public Sector Digest.

Diane was born with the gift of encouragement and the desire for everyone around her to meet their potential. Her core belief is that as social beings, we flourish in healthy, sustainable communities where good governance, servant leadership, and compassionate culture support the well-being of all.

Over the past 30 years, this conviction has taken Diane to countless communities in leadership roles from community organizer, television producer, and entrepreneur to local government chief administrative officer.

Today, her firm Kalen Consulting provides expert advisory services to community leaders, while subsidiary Kalen Academy offers civic leadership training.

Diane is a graduate of the University of Toronto's Trinity College with a Bachelor of Arts joint specialist degree in political science and philosophy and holds a Master of Arts degree from York University of Victoria and is a certified municipal clerk with the International Association of Municipal Clerks.

DianeKalenSukra.com

@dianekalensukra

SaveYourCity.ca

WORKBOOK, RESOURCES & TOOLS

Printed in the USA
CPSIA information can be obtained
at www.ICGtesting.com
CBHW021126170424
7072CB00002B/88